FOREWORD
by Lord Phillips of Sudbury

The idea behind this book is an inspired one – to celebrate the so-called ordinary buildings of Sudbury. A quick glance reveals that every property illustrated has its own distinct charm and interest. Such buildings complement the star, listed ones, and provide the context within which they are best appreciated. Sir John Betjeman made this very point when he wrote 40 years ago to support the (successful) efforts to reverse the planning consent for demolition of the Corn Exchange on the Market Hill.

The planners, of course, have to juggle with many conflicting priorities, sometimes to alarming effect. For example, since the war the Town Council has contemplated a relief road joining Cross Street and Melford Road via the grounds of Walnuttree Hospital and across The Croft; has nearly adopted an inner ring road which would have destroyed about 90 properties and the amenity of many more; has sanctioned the destruction of the magnificent stepped terrace of 18 weavers houses, Inkerman Row, as well as North Street School, in both cases to make room for parking.

In heightening the visual awareness of the public, as this book splendidly will, it encourages good new building no less than retention of what is worthwhile from the past. It will, for example, awaken appreciation of window design, suitable street furniture, good proportions, harmonious materials and sympathetic colours. The famous Sudbury bricks, particularly are displayed in their silver grey glory.

Most Sudburians are mighty fond – nay proud – of their town. This book will make them more so, but also more vigilant of the whole fabric of their special town.

David Burnett and his design collaborator, Robin Drury, deserve great praise.

Andrew Phillips

Published by The Sudbury Society
c/o 157 Melford Road, Sudbury CO10 1JU

Copyright © The Sudbury Society 2002
All rights reserved. No part of this publication may be reproduced, stored in a retrieval system or transmitted in any form or by any means, electronic, mechanical, photocopying, recording or otherwise without the prior consent of the copyright owner.

THE SUDBURY SOCIETY
The Society is an Amenity Society serving Sudbury and District, registered with the Civic Trust. Further information about the work of the Society and membership can be found on the Society's website at www.sudburysociety.co.uk or by contacting the Society's Membership Secretary, Marion Hopps, "Cygnets" 31 Church Street, Sudbury CO10 2BL

ISBN No. 0-9543398-0-0

Photography & Text – David Burnett
Design & Layout – Robin Drury, Radius Design
Print – The Wolsey Press, Ipswich

cover picture:
North House and 28 The Croft, Sudbury

AUTHOR'S NOTE

Many people have helped with this publication. Given the number of properties involved it was not possible to visit every one but I would first like to express my thanks to all those local people who welcomed me into their properties and allowed me to look into dark attics or pore over old title deeds in an attempt to untangle the history of their houses.

My thanks also to those people who assisted with the research or helped by providing additional photographs or other illustrative material for publication. The latter group includes in particular John Bridges, Maureen and Alan Bloys, Hugh Belsey of Gainsborough's House, Alan Cocksedge, Kathleen Grimwood, Stephen Hough, David Tooth of Vanners Ltd and John Turkentine. Special thanks are due here to John Rodger Brown whose architectural camera coped with a number of large buildings in narrow streets that had defeated my own photographic efforts.

I exercised my own judgement on which buildings merited inclusion, using the broad criteria set out in the Introduction. Readers are bound to disagree with particular inclusions or feel that there are buildings that I should have included. Such disagreement is both inevitable and extremely healthy and you are very welcome to contact me with your views.

Again I have striven for accuracy in what I have said about the age and past history of buildings but there are bound to be some errors of fact and interpretation. Again I would welcome further information from readers.

The book could not have been published in this extensive and highly illustrated format without very generous financial support from Babergh District Council, the Community Energy Project, Sudbury Freemen's Trust, Sudbury Town Council and Suffolk County Council (Cllr. Nick Irwin's Locality Budget). My sincere thanks to all these grant awarding bodies and also to Thorntons Estate Agents for sponsoring the map.

Finally I am endebted to both my wife Val for her work on proof reading and to Robin Drury of Radius Design who laboured for many hours to translate my raw text and photographs into an attractive reality.

David Burnett
Chairman, The Sudbury Society
June 2002

INTRODUCTION

"The historic environment.... is central to how we see ourselves and to our identity as individuals, communities and as a nation. It is a collective memory, containing an infinity of stories, some ancient, some recent; stories written in stone, brick, wood, glass, steel.

It is as fragile as it is precious. It is not renewable. If we fail to protect and sustain it we risk losing permanently not just the fabric itself, but the history of which it is the visible expression."

from 'The Historic Environment; a force for our future' DCMS/DTLR Dec 2001

Sudbury is an old market town with a history of continuous settlement that stretches back at least 1200 years; our distinctive and attractive townscape is thus a mix of buildings from many periods. Most local people are aware of the fine old buildings in the town dating from the 15th through to the early 19th Century, for example the three fine medieval churches, the wool merchants' houses on Stour Street and the elegant Georgian town houses in Friars Street. These and many other old buildings in Sudbury are considered to be of such national architectural or historic interest that they have been given a statutory Grade I or Grade II listing.

However, we strongly believe that many other unlisted buildings in Sudbury also contribute to the unique variety and character of the local townscape. For example many striking local properties were built in the Victorian and Edwardian eras and they feature very prominently in this Local List. These buildings co-exist remarkably well with the older listed buildings in the town. Perhaps this is because most retain the simple "Classical" proportions of the earlier Georgian period - local builders and their clients generally had no time for the wilder excesses of Gothic revival! In addition, until the 1920's, builders were still using local bricks, both reds and whites, which helped new buildings to harmonise with the old.

Generally we chose to include buildings which form an attractive or interesting element in the local street scene, either individually or as part of a group, and which have retained much of their original appearance. Others may have been selected primarily for their local historical significance and we have tried to give, where appropriate, information about what a building was formerly used for and who once lived there. In addition to buildings we have also included various items of street furniture - post boxes, milestones, water troughs, iron drain grilles, railings and walls which also form part of the street scene and contribute to local distinctiveness and character.

The Sudbury townscape is constantly changing; clearly this publication is a snap shot at a particular point in time. Even in the few months between writing and publication some buildings have been altered or given a new colour, and the former Gas Works office in Meadow Lane has been demolished.

Many visitors to our "launch" Exhibition at the Town Hall in September 2001 commented that they had previously been unaware of the very existence of many of these buildings and asked us to publish a book on them. We hope that this publication will encourage local people to look again at familiar parts of the town and particularly upward! More generally the book should help to stimulate a greater awareness both of the rich diversity of the townscape and the way in which local buildings reflect the past history of the town and its residents.

We know that the vast majority of the owners of the buildings featured in our publication take pride in their properties and will continue to look after them with care and sensitivity. However properties change hands and our hope is that that by identifying and celebrating these buildings in a Local List we are flagging up their importance and so helping to ensure their survival for future generations of townspeople to enjoy.

These buildings should not be regarded as a "third eleven" compared to Grade I & II properties in the town but an essential and important part of Sudbury's building heritage and places where generations of former townspeople worked and lived.

The Sudbury Society – July 2002

CONTENTS

chapter		page
	Foreword by Lord Phillips of Sudbury	i
	Author's note	ii
	Introduction	iii
1	Ballingdon and Brundon	2
2	Cross Street to Stour Street	9
3	Church Street	17
4	Plough Lane to School Street	20
5	Friars Street	26
6	Priory Walk to Meadow Lane	31
7	Station Road	36
8	Great Eastern Road, Cornard and Newton Roads	46
9	East Street and Waldingfield Road	51
10	Market Hill to Gaol Lane	58
11	Gainsborough Street to Gregory Street	61
12	The Croft and Church Walk	65
13	Around Acton Square	70
14	New Street and Prince Street	74
15	North Street	80
16	Girling Street to Queens Road	83
17	Melford Road - west side	88
18	Melford Road - east side	93
19	Priory Road	100
	Map	102
	Index	103

Sudbury, Suffolk
the unlisted heritage

A visual celebration of Sudbury's unlisted architectural legacy by David Burnett

Published by The Sudbury Society
with support from Babergh District Council, The Community Energy Project,
Sudbury Freemen's Trust, Sudbury Town Council and Suffolk County Council

Chapter 1 – BALLINGDON & BRUNDON

MIDDLETON ROAD

Detail of No.25

11-41 Middleton Road

These cottages form an attractive group with their pantiled roofs and colour rendered walls. Many retain iron railings which may be original. The cottages probably date from the 1840's. In the 1851 Census they were lived in by a mix of brickmakers, hand loom weavers, lime burners and agricultural labourers. Many must have worked for Allens who owned the brickfields, lime kilns and maltings further along the road towards Middleton.

BULMER ROAD

7 End Cottage,

An attractive timber framed, peg tiled cottage, probably 17thC. The original front door was where the small window is now, opening straight off the street. Neighbouring properties to the left also contain old timbers but No 7 retains its period feel.

BALLINGDON & BRUNDON

BULMER ROAD

14 Bulmer Road
This Victorian house of 1879 dominates the corner with Brundon Lane. In 1891 Thomas Bareham lived here. He managed the nearby Victoria Brickworks (now the location of the industrial estate). Note the heavy triangular moulded lintels above the original sash windows - similar lintels can be seen on other houses by the local builder, Edwin Coote Green, whose initials appear on the datestone.

10 Bulmer Road
It is easy to miss this cottage as you visit the tip! Built in the 18th/early 19thC of warm red brick and clay peg tiles its hedge screen give it a rural ambience. The recessing of the door and ground floor windows within shallow brick arches adds to its visual appeal. The wing on the right is a modern but sympathetic addition. Walter Smith lived here in 1891. He managed the brickworks which lay immediately to the left of the cottage.

Chapter 1 – BALLINGDON & BRUNDON

VALLEY WALK

BRUNDON

Railway Bridge
The railway came to Sudbury in 1849; this bridge dates from 1865 when the line was extended to Cambridge. The bridge carries Brundon Lane over The Valley Walk at an angle of about 45 degrees. This angle was a severe test for the skill of the bricklayers; the detail photo shows how magnificently they responded.

Stone Cottage, Brundon
Most properties in Brundon are listed but not Stone Cottage behind the Hall. The combination of flint and warm red brick is delightful and even the asbestos roof has acquired a covering of lichen. The core of the cottage with heavy internal timbers is on the right - 17thC or earlier. The section on the left is later, perhaps added as a stable and hayloft. The farm bailiff, Robert Woodhouse, appears to have been living here in 1871.

BALLINGDON & BRUNDON

BALLINGDON STREET – north west side

The Red Onion
This was the local Mission Hall, built by the Plymouth Brethren in 1877. Older residents may remember it when it was the local garage in the 1970's (Eric Kinnard & Son.) It forms an attractive group with the attached house and the birch trees.

67 & 68-70 Ballingdon Street
The front of No 67 (Letterston Cottage on the left) suggests a date around 1840 but a timber framed rear cross wing indicates something much earlier. Similarly Nos 68-70 may look Victorian but the steep peg tiled roof and the exposed purlins in the north east gable show that there is an earlier core. It was once a single property which may have been owned by the 17thC family of clothiers, the Ruggles.

BALLINGDON & BRUNDON

BALLINGDON STREET – north west side

Former Refuse and Sewage Works - 1903
Gone is the Refuse Works which once dominated this part of town with its tall chimney. However the Sewage Pumping Station survives as an embodiment of local civic pride and a fine example of the use of local red and white bricks.

south east side

Horse trough
A relic from a more leisurely age. Supplied by the Metropolitan Drinking Fountain and Cattle Trough Association and erected by Edward Arnold, Mayor, to commemorate the Coronation of George V in 1911. Dogs drank from the stone tray below and passers-by from the spout at the end nearest the railway bridge - note the brass staple where a cup was once attached.

BALLINGDON & BRUNDON

BALLINGDON STREET – *south east side*

21-22 Ballingdon Street
The irregular arrangement of windows and doors provides visual interest and also hints at the former commercial use of this house. In the late 19th/early 20thC the Berry family ran a bakery here at No 22 and a dairy in the linked property at the back - No 21.

51-53 Ballingdon Street
No 51 on the left is a fine early 19thC property which adds dignity and grace to this corner. The continuous curve of the brick facade is particularly noteworthy as is the doorway. In 1891 Ann Shepard, widow and beerhouse keeper, lived here. It was then The Queens Head pub. Next door is No 53 Hickbush Cottage, originally two early 19thC cottages - note the blocked doorway on the far right. The two blank windows are probably an original feature, designed to maintain the rhythm of the facade rather than an attempt to avoid the Window Tax.

Forge House, 24 Ballingdon Street
No 24 is the right hand part of what was once a single timber framed house. The photo shows the former smithy at the side of No 24, also timber framed with early brick and cobble floors. It may well date back to the late 17thC when records show that Thomas Wright, blacksmith, worked here. It is therefore of considerable local historical interest.

BALLINGDON STREET – *south east side*

Talas House, 47-48 Ballingdon Street

A striking range of buildings, once the offices and public house of Mauldons White Horse Brewery and now adding character and variety to the local streetscape. The oriel windows and small upper window panes are characteristic of the Edwardian era - they were rebuilt after a fire in May 1900. Mauldons owned many other local pubs including The Anchor in Friars Street, which still has their name in its frosted glass windows.

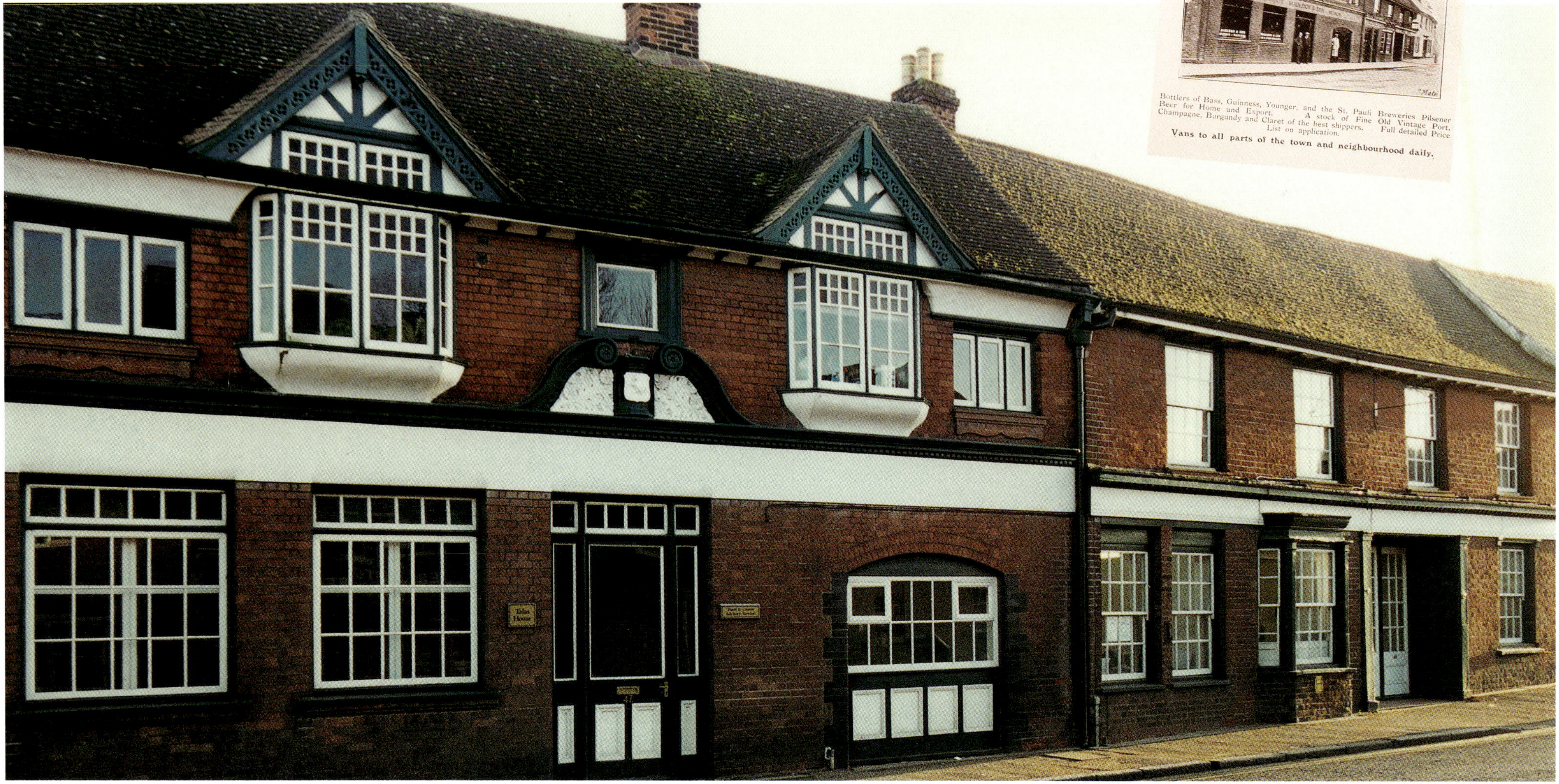

Chapter 2 – CROSS STREET to STOUR STREET

CROSS STREET – east side

5-9 Cross Street

A terrace of well proportioned, early 19thC town houses. The blank window spaces above the doorways give rhythm to the terrace and the local white brick has weathered very attractively. At the north end No 5 (extreme left) is larger than the others but still seems to be part of the overall design. John Spring, a butcher, lived here in 1879 and it may well have been his shop as well. At the south end No 9 (green door) has its original boot scraper on the top step. Some modern windows in the terrace but it has an overall group value.

30-31 Cross Street

Many brick, three storey silk weavers' cottages survive in the town dating from the third quarter of the 19thC. Here No 31, on the right, has the characteristic "straight through" first floor room with large windows front and back to give maximum light. However this pair is much older than the other weavers' cottages and has a timber framed construction. Certainly pre 1825 the pair may even be late 18thC.

CROSS STREET – *east side*

32 Cross Street

Where there is now a very large first floor window there was once a loading door with a hoist above. This was a Victorian granary serving the brewery which was linked with The Bull. The granary was probably built c.1868 by the brewer Stephen Spurgin. About 1885 the Brewery was taken over by Mauldons. Included for local historical interest.

The Bull Inn – Cross Street frontage

The Bull Inn is an ancient, listed timber framed property but the Listing description makes no mention of these buildings at the rear. The timber framed cross wing on the right appears 16th or early 17thC - the steep pitch of the roof is noteworthy whilst the ventilator in the roof suggests that it may have been used for malting. The brick and tiled extension to the left was probably a brewhouse, built by Stephen Spurgin in 1869 – his initials and the date are on the side of the tall chimney.

CROSS STREET – *east side*

36 Cross Street
Following major work on the facade in 1999 this shop now sits elegantly at this important road junction, forming a pleasing group with Nos 37 and 38. The inside is well worth a visit - look at the way the main beams converge to fit the house into its wedge-shaped site. Probably 17thC with a Victorian brick front. In the late 19th/early 20thC this was a grocers shop. After WW2 it had a brief life as The Riverside Hotel (then incorporating No 37 next door).

37 Cross Street
A well proportioned early 19thC house, c1830-40. The use of red pantiles on a domestic house is, if original, quite unusual for Sudbury. The large doorway to the right led to the coach house - by contrast a very common feature with the larger houses in the town.

38 Cross Street, Bridge House
No 38 complements and contrasts with its neighbour. The slate roof with terracotta ridge tiles, imposing double bay window and original cast iron railings are all attractive features. Built about 1860 it was occupied at various times by the local Baptist minister and the undertaker to the Ipswich Cooperative Society - the mortuary was on land at the rear accessed from Church Street.

BRIDGE FOOT

5 Bridge Foot

Old Sudbury had a maze of alleyways and courtyards behind many of the street frontages. Bridge Foot is a good surviving example, lying on your left as you approach Ballingdon Bridge from the town. No 5 was originally two timber framed cottages, probably 17thC, but fronted in brick in the 19thC. In 1891 a brickyard labourer, George Reeve, lived in No 5.

CROSS STREET – west side

61 Cross Street

It forms an attractive pair with No 62 (on the right). The elegant ground floor facade may well date from the 1870's when Mrs Mary Ann Cahill ran "dining rooms" and then a shop here. The sashes are original and the pair probably date from the mid 19thC.

79 & 85 Cross Street – summerhouses

These attractive summerhouses overlook the mill stream and Freemen's Little Common. Both have been much restored in recent years but in origin they probably date back to the 18thC. Indeed the right hand one may be the very "banqueting or summerhouse" which is referred to in a document of 1707 as owned by the clothier Samuel Griggs. He lived at No 78.

CROSS STREET — west side

82 & 83 Cross Street
This was originally a short terrace of three cottages, built in 1834. By 1871 they were occupied by Walter Turkentine, blacksmith, Mary Foakes, charwoman and Sarah Cobham, straw plaiter.
The walls of the cottages consist of a studwork frame, filled with lath and plaster. A series of heavy exposed joists support the first floor. These cottages are included because they contribute to the rich diversity of the architecture in Cross Street and also show how traditional timber framed construction methods continued well into the 19thC.

Spread Eagle, public house
The pub is now a sad sight with its windows shuttered and signs removed. It dates from about 1870 when Ann Amey, beer seller, lived here and it was already known as the Spread Eagle. The ground floor facia and the massive chimney stack are significant elements in the street scene yet plans have been approved for the fascia to be removed, all the original windows and doors replaced and the size of the chimney drastically reduced. The remaining shell will then be converted into three cottages. The Society deplores this loss of the building's historic identity. The second photo shows the smithy behind the pub c1925 with Robert Turkentine at work.

GARDEN PLACE

CROSS STREET & MILL HILL – *north side*

102 Cross Street

A mid 19thC house with simple, uncluttered proportions. Like Hill House next door No 102 is on land owned by the Daking family in the early 19thC. By 1847 they owed £8000 to their local bankers with their extensive property portfolio as security. In that year the bankers lost patience and put the property up for sale. At the time there were only outbuildings on this plot and the house must have been built soon after the auction.

8 Garden Place

This attractive cottage (combining two former cottages) is part of the terrace behind the Spread Eagle. Many people know it best from the meadows where the terrace backs onto the mill stream. The large first floor windows of No 8 show that hand loom weavers lived and worked in some of these cottages; indeed there were also two small silk factories in this row. In 1903 Reginald Warner's Gainsborough Silk Weaving Company began life in Garden Place before transferring to Priory Walk, (see P31).

27 Mill Hill, Hill House

A substantial, well proportioned early 19thC house, built about 1820 by Robert Daking on a site which was then connected with the tanning trade. The elegant doorcase with reeding and panelling adds dignity to the facade. The three storey extension to the rear can be dated post 1893 and is probably Edwardian. Many cottages once lined Mill Hill: now this is the only surviving house with a Mill Hill address.

WALNUT TREE LANE – *south east side*

An unusual garden feature at the back of The Granary - a niche set into the 18thC wall which once bounded the grounds of Springfield Lodge (the large house next door, where Isaac Clover lived in the late 19thC).

37 Walnut Tree Lane, The Granary

Isaac Clover's late 19thC granary stands opposite his grand four storey roller mill (now part of the Mill Hotel). Grain was stored in a tall silo attached to the granary and then fed down through an overhead pipe across the lane and into the mill. The ground floor, now offices, was once used as stabling and there is some interesting, much earlier brickwork internally. The west wall bears evidence of having housed a 'lucum' (hoist box), now bricked up. This is also illustrated in the photograph, probably taken in the early 1890's. See how much The Mill and The Granary have changed since then.

Riverside Cottage

A pair of back to back houses built by the miller, Isaac Clover, in 1880. His initials appear on the datestone. The simple functional lines and the steep peg tiled roof create quite an impressive building.

15

WALNUT TREE LANE

Walnuttree Hospital

This powerful and imposing neo-Tudor building was the Sudbury Union Workhouse, opened in 1837 at a cost of £7110 on a site once occupied by Simon of Sudbury's College. The original architect and builder was John Brown of Norwich: he built the central core with many of the wings to east and west being added in later years. The workhouse served Sudbury and 41 other parishes both in Essex and Suffolk, an area of 119 square miles. The stern regime within its walls made these "Bastilles" places of dread for Victorian paupers.

In 1929 it was taken over by West Suffolk C.C. and it evolved into a local hospital. However, some of the former workhouse residents continued to live there. The last of these "workhouse women" was Lily Ambrose, born in 1898, sent to

the workhouse in 1914 because she was carrying an illegitimate child and finally passing away in the Walnuttree in 1985, still clasping the doll she had held since her own baby was taken from her at birth.

For both good and ill this building has been part of the life of our area for over 150 years. It is a vast construction in Sudbury terms and the quality of much of the design is extremely high. When Sudbury has its new hospital, this site will probably be redeveloped for housing. A capable and imaginative architect should be given the brief to retain much of the existing building and design any new elements to blend with it, as was done very successfully at the Long Melford maltings.

STOUR STREET

Kentish Lodge, Stour Street

A substantial Victorian villa built about 1870 for George Whorlow who was clearly a man of substance. A Trade Directory of 1864 describes him as a carrier to London and as sole agent to the Great Eastern Railway Company, presumably responsible for organising the shipment of goods between Sudbury and London by rail. The family business also dealt in coal and lime and by the turn of the century they were also advertising a local removal service.

Chapter 3 CHURCH STREET – *south east side*

8-11 Church Street

A short terrace of substantial and well proportioned mid 19thC town houses, white brick at the front, red at sides and rear. Most have their original sash windows although the visual effect would be improved if the owners could agree on one colour for the wooden eaves of the terrace. In 1888 No 8 (on the left) was owned by the umbrella silk manufacturers, Kipling, Dennler and Company, and probably used as a base for their outworkers. In 1893 they opened a new power driven factory in the Cornard Road - now Stephen Walters' mill (see p47).

32-33 Church Street

A pair of late 19thC cottages opposite the Bull Inn, built in a highly individual style. Note the projecting bays with mock Tudor timberwork and the use of contrasting red brick to construct a castle motif around the twin doorways. Eccentric but fun!

17

CHURCH STREET – *north west side*

37-42 Church Street, All Saints Terrace

It is very rare to find a Victorian terrace in this condition, with all the original doors and windows surviving. Three of the highly ornate door knockers also survive, along with the iron gate to the central passageway. The datestone reads AM & CEM 1889 - Ann and Christie Mauldon owned the Bull Inn and brewery next door and they built the cottages to rent out. The decorated stone lintels and door arches are characteristic of this late Victorian date. On the extreme right is No 42, the side of which faces into All Saints churchyard. White brick gives way to red to match the existing cottages there.

44 Church Street

This was once two cottages known as 43 and 44 Churchyard. The heavy nail studded doors and the square hood moulds above the windows are striking features. The cottages may well be 17thC in origin and we believe that they were given this Tudor brick facelift in the mid 19thC when Charles Badham was the vicar of All Saints. The Vicarage was also restored at that time and linked with the cottages by a fine brick wall (to the right of the cottage - look for the curious recess in this wall).

46 Church Street, Vine Cottage

An attractive peg tiled and timber framed cottage, possibly 17thC. The arrangement of the windows and the central chimney stack suggest that it may once have been two cottages.

CHURCH STREET – *north west side*

49-50 Church Street,
The window sashes indicate a late 19thC date but the steep pitch of the peg tiled roof suggests that it may have begun life as an older timber framed building. However inside there are no old timbers visible. Whatever their age the cottages, with their contrasting colour washed walls, now make an attractive pair.

Baptist Church
A superb Gothic Revival church in the Early English style. It cost £2000 and was built in 1889 by the local builders, Grimwood and Son; the architect was William Eade FRIBA. It replaced the earlier church which was too small and in need of repair. The lines are strong, even muscular. The rose window in the gable, with its tinted diamond panes, is very fine. It would be interesting to know whether a local blacksmith was employed to make the ornamental door hinges and the delicate iron railings.

CHURCH STREET - *north west side*

54 Church Street

The fine doorcase and windows frames suggest an early 19thC date but appearances are deceptive. The house is timber framed with beamed ceilings on the ground floor and two short cross wings to the rear. The extra width of the left hand window reflects the time when it was a local shop. At the time of the 1891 Census John Heard, general dealer and common lodging house keeper, owned the property and there were eight lodgers in residence. On the left side of the house is a passageway which once led to the five cottages of Spooners Yard. There are old stories about a dancing bear being led through the passage - perhaps the showman was staying at the lodging house!

Chapter 4 – PLOUGH LANE to SCHOOL STREET

Plough Lane (Nos 1-7 and 21-36)

Rows of red brick early Victorian cottages follow the narrow curving line of this medieval lane. Unsurprisingly, some of them contain the remains of older timber framed buildings. A few cottages have painted walls or modern replacement windows but not to the point of affecting the overall attractiveness of the lane, particularly now that many of the overhead wires have been put underground. We therefore feel that all the properties from Straw Lane to Stour Street have an overall group value. A few are now selected for particular comment.

PLOUGH LANE – *north west side*

21 Plough Lane

An attractive, rendered brick house with a tiled roof. It is probably 18thC in origin and in the early 19thC was owned by a member of the Constable family. A few older people may remember it as Kirby's Dairy. The cows were brought from the meadows into Stour Street, down the cobbled surface of Plough Lane and in through the double doors for milking. The window beyond those doors slid back to allow the sale of milk and butter. (The previous photo on p20, giving a general view of the Lane, shows how the owner of No 22 has a flying freehold above the front door and hall of No 21 - quite common in Sudbury).

23

24

22

22, 23 & 24 Plough Lane

These are the first three cottages in the photo on page 20. The internal flash photos suggest that these cottages might have once been parts of a single merchant's house with No 22 on the site of the parlour, No 23 being the surviving hall and No 24 on the site of the service end. No 23 (middle) has a full timber frame although the roof has been renewed. The only old timber remaining in No 22 (left) is the other side of the same stud wall seen in No 23. No 22 might have been the parlour of the merchant's house - the owner decorated the wall to give the impression of high status wooden panelling. Unfortunately the decoration only survives on the vertical studs. The other photo (right) shows the cross passage which still survives between Nos 23 and 24. The two blocked doors on the right led into the pantry and buttery.

21

PLOUGH LANE – *south east side*

STRAW LANE – *north east side*

Ivy Lodge

The photos show very different aspects of the house. From the side view the two steep gables indicate that it is timber framed, possibly dating back to the 15thC - it has a substantial crown post roof. The brick facade and entrance on Straw Lane was clearly added at some considerable expense to modernise the house. The deep eaves suggest a date of around 1830 for this facelift which was almost certainly the work of Thomas Ginn who designed the Town Hall and owned Ivy Lodge at that time. The brick arch of the doorway is very fine with each brick tapered to fit.

A fascinating building for the House Detectives!

7 Plough Lane

No 7 has absorbed the former Nos 8 and 9. The warm red brickwork and the panelled double door-case suggest an early 19thC date. However in the attic there are sooted beams indicating it began life as a 15thC medieval open hall with a floor being inserted in the 16thC to make it a two storey building. Some local people may remember sitting below this beamed ceiling when this was the Rising Sun public house. Beyond No 7 is the NW end of Ivy Lodge. Note how the first floor is jettied out over Plough Lane. It is likely that No 7 and Ivy Lodge were once one large merchant's house. Brewers Map of Sudbury 1714 appears to confirm this, showing "Mr Hovells house" occupying this whole corner site.

22

STRAW LANE – *north east side*

The Coach House and The Trap House

These photos show buildings which originally housed the carriages of local residents whilst the upper floors were used as hay lofts. The top picture shows the white brick Coach House which is Victorian and belonged to Ivy Lodge. Below, the red brick Trap House appears to be early 19thC and once belonged to Trinity House, the former manse of the United Reform Church in School Street. Both have been successfully converted to domestic use and now add interest and variety to the local street scene.

2-5 Straw Lane

These simple mid 19thC cottages also contribute to the charm of the lane. On September 4th 1873 Grace Lilley, the owner of Ivy Lodge and these cottages, responded coolly to an order from the Town Council to connect the cottages to the town water supply: "I beg to inform you that there is a very good supply of water belonging to them from which pump I always use water for my own table." The outcome of this dispute is not recorded.

STRAW LANE – *south west side*

8-11 *Straw Lane*

These are possibly the oldest brick cottages in the town. They were built by Thomas Green after he signed a 79 year lease on this patch of waste ground on 2nd June 1832. It was a condition of the lease that he built "four tenements or dwelling houses" within a year. No 8 (extreme left) shows that insensitive changes to a building can sometimes be reversed. A few years ago it was marred by aluminium windows and the warm red bricks had been painted. Today after a great deal of hard work, particularly to remove the paint, the unity and appeal of this terrace has been restored.

On the right is the mellow red brick wall to the garden of Trinity House - another fine feature of the local townscape.

SCHOOL STREET

1 School Street
A small red brick and peg tiled cottage to the left of the United Reform Church. It appears to be mid 19thC but the modern lean to extension at the side is not a thing of beauty.

36 School Street
This property stands opposite the cottage and abuts the medieval merchant's houses in Stour Street .The central doorway onto School Street is curiously small compared to the flanking Victorian sash windows. The steep peg tiled roof and the relationship of the property to the merchant's houses suggest that it may have an earlier timber framed core.

14-24 School Street
These Victorian cottages have been restored with great sensitivity. They feature an attractive and unusual combination of flint and white brick. The four blank windows and the detailing below the eaves add to the visual interest, particularly with a low winter sun. The gardens are a picture in summer!

Chapter 5 FRIARS STREET – *south east side*

1-3 Friars Street

An imposing Victorian shopping development comprising two shops on the ground floor with accommodation and offices above. The deep bold carving of the stylised leaves on the pilasters and the crisp detail of the brickwork are striking features. The large curved glass windows on the corner of the building show just how far glass making techniques advanced during the 19thC. In 1888 Charles Emmerson, clothier and pawnbroker, occupied No 1 (now James Cox) and Henry Westrope, grocer, No 3 (now the Thai Restaurant).

19 Friars Street, Bentley House

This attractive property lies behind Buzzards Hall and is reached down a narrow access path from the Street. The date 1840 and the initials of three members of the Ray family appear high up beneath the deep eaves. The front door has an excellent panelled doorcase with a rectangular fanlight, the glazing bars forming a cross. This design feature also appears on the two sets of French windows to the garden. The various blank windows were intended to give rhythm and balance to the house. It was named after the late 19thC Congo missionary, Holman Bentley, who stayed here with the Misses Ray when on furlough.

FRIARS STREET – *south east side*

47 Friars Street, Barton Cottage

Outwardly No 47 appears to be an early Victorian house with wooden casement windows replacing the original sashes. The exterior has a quiet dignity but the real interest lies inside. If you enter the courtyard of the Angel Inn on the left you will see many old timbers along the side and rear of No 47, evidence that the Victorian brick facade conceals a much older building. The front section of the house appears to be the two bay cross wing of a larger merchant's house, possibly dating back to the 15thC. (The neighbouring properties, Nos 49 and 51, may incorporate other elements of this larger house.) No 47 also has a later 17thC extension at the rear. Traditionally the cottage is linked with the Barton family but this needs further research.

The Cricket Ground railings

A fine set of late Victorian railings which has both visual and historical significance. The individual wrought iron railings are set into a cast iron plate which in turn is mounted on the low brick wall. The maker's name, Barton and Co., shows that they were made by the local iron works in Station Road, probably for the ground's opening in 1891. The firm became Bruntons Propellers in about 1914.

63 Friars Street

An elegant well proportioned town house c1840. By this time local white brick, although expensive, was more fashionable than red and was used for the visible fronts of properties. Here red brick was retained for the sides and rear of the house. Both the tapered brick arch above the attractive fanlight and the ground floor shutters add to its appeal.

FRIARS STREET – north west side

8 Friars Street
This building is noteworthy for its fine brick detailing and impression of height and solidity. The Victorian shopfront seems virtually untouched and there are many interesting features behind the wide front door. This seems to have been purpose built as a butcher's shop - William Burch was working here in 1879; by 1888 Austen Blandon owned the business. The wide front door allowed whole carcases to be carried in from the street. Inside there are ventilation openings in the wall and some old iron hooks on the heavy ceiling beams. Below, in the cellar, there is still the original walk-in cold store.

8c Friars Street, Anchor Cottage
Anchor Cottage lies behind the street in the Anchor car park. This timber framed and peg tiled building may well date back to the 17thC. It has been suggested that it was once part of a larger outbuilding of the Anchor which was used as a theatre in the early 19thC. The famous tightrope walker, Blondin, gave a display in the adjacent yard on July 1st 1872, including pushing a passenger in a wheelbarrow along a suspended rope.

FRIARS STREET – north west side

22 Friars Street

This impressive building reflects the wealth and importance of the Independent congregation who built it as their minister's manse in 1859. It must have needed an army of servants to run it! The Chapel next door was demolished in 1964 to make way for the Social Services offices. The use of broken pediments to frame the arched sash windows in the two gables contributes to the overall classical feel of the building.

10-12 Friars Street

This fine late Victorian range is now a bookshop. It seems to have been built originally as two shops with accommodation above - shop keepers still lived over the shop then. By 1908 it had become one shop, a confectioners owned by Josiah Berry and Son. The canvas canopy protects the books from the sun but also makes it difficult for passers by to see the first storey which is well worth studying. Note the elegant wooden window cases and the moulded brick detailing on the window lintels and string courses, all seemingly as crisp today as when the property was built. At ground level look for the cast iron grilles below the display windows which give some air and light to the cellars below.

FRIARS STREET – north west side

70 Friars Street

The house was built between 1823 and 1832 by James Sillitoe the younger, a local carpenter and builder. Sillitoe was also responsible for building the two storey stable and gig house on the right of the entrance (with the semi-circular windows). Benjamin Bloys bought the property in 1867 and established his mineral water business here, doubtless profiting from the growth of the Temperance movement! The early 20thC photo shows George Bloys on the left, an unknown employee, Benjamin Macro Bloys and Mr. Challis up on their delivery waggon. The single storey building in the courtyard was the bottling works and indeed, some of the overhead drive shafts, pulleys and belts can still be seen inside. The three oriel windows and hanging tiles were added to the house in the early 20thC. These three buildings form an interesting and attractive group on this prominent corner site opposite the Priory gateway.

Victorian Post Box (no.1002)

Street furniture can make a significant contribution to the townscape. In this case it is a positive one! The use of moulded red bricks to frame the box in the wall of No 58 is pleasing but it is a shame that this old feature has been so neglected by the Post Office.

Chapter 6 PRIORY WALK to MEADOW LANE — *This section covers a network of lanes lying between Friars Street and The Valley Walk*

PRIORY WALK

Victorian Stay Factory

This building has an ugly extension facing onto Priory Walk but the back reveals this more attractive aspect. The factory seems to date from the early 1880's and to have been first occupied by the Ipswich based firm of stay and corset makers, Footman, Pretty and Nicholson. In 1906 Reginald Warner established his silk weaving firm here which grew to become Gainsborough Silk Weaving Company. The early photo shows him inside the building. Important because of its local historical links.

The Old Priory

This cottage is marked on Jeremy Nicholl's Survey Map of the Priory Estate drawn in 1734. It has undergone much extension and modernisation both inside and out but the timber framed core of the house seems to date back to the 17thC, after the Dissolution of the Priory. However, excavations in 1969 in the garden and the surrounding area revealed a well and foundations of walls, that were probably monastic.

31

QUAY LANE - *east side*

4 Quay Lane
Until the 1960's these were two cottages; there are still two front doors on the North side. The walls are timber framed with lath and plaster infill and the general proportions suggest an 18thC date. The roof contains a number of old timbers but these were probably reused from a demolished earlier building. Although internally the doorways are very low and "cottagey" this may well have started out as one substantial house and subsequently been divided up into cottages.

1 Quay Lane
No 1 exists in a kind of listing limbo. The gabled left hand section, directly on the lane, is listed, (although wrongly described as part of 51 Friars Street) but the other part of the house, the cross wing on the right, is not. Clearly the whole group of timber framed buildings dates back to the 17thC or earlier and the listing details need to be updated. Visually this frontage to Quay Lane is extremely satisfying.

QUAY LANE - *east side*

The old Boathouse
Sudbury Boat Club was founded in 1880. The boathouse does not appear on the 1887 O.S. map but is shown in 1904. The weather boarded walls and felted roof have no particular visual interest but inside the heavy timber framework which supports both the roof and boats stored there, is quite spectacular featuring a tie beam and king post construction.

The Cricket Pavilion
In 1891 Sudbury Cricket Club moved here from their field on Nonsuch Meadow and George Grimwood and Son built this pavilion the following year. Originally tiled, it was later thatched and then in the 1980's tiled again and extended. However, the original central core remains, including shutters which lift up for attachment to projecting supports. This arrangement can be seen in the atmospheric early photo from the 1890's.

33

RED HOUSE LANE - west side

The Cottage
Although the gazebo and serpentine walls of Red House are listed, no one thought to include this attractive peg tiled and weatherboarded outbuilding. The projecting mansard roof is supported on heavy joists and arched braces. Although now residential, it may originally have been a stable with hayloft above.

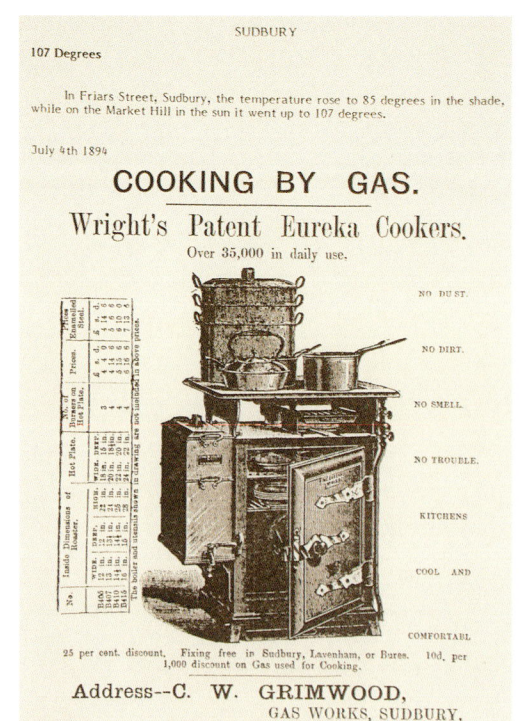

MEADOW LANE

Former Gas Works offices
All that survives today of Sudbury's town gas works which was opened in 1835. These offices stand at the western end of the lane. They were built c1900 but copied the classical triangular pediment and round arches of their Regency predecessor. Why in Sudbury are so many worhwhile buildings like this being swept away rather than being incorporated into modern redevelopments?

34

MEADOW LANE - north side

MEADOW LANE - south side

2 Meadow Lane

There is a completely different feel to Meadow Lodge on the opposite corner which looks like a Grimwood design. Note the prominent gables and the use of contrasting white brick for the detailing - lintels, quoins and string courses. It dates from about 1900 and was once the home of the Cundy family, who were local florists, nurserymen and seed merchants. From 1926 to 1963 they owned the nearby warehouse between Hamilton and Francis Roads which, sadly, was demolished in 2001.

1 Meadow Lane

A substantial house, c1840, with a classical feel to the simple doorcase. The curved corner wall is a fine example of the skills of local bricklayers - note the switch to the shorter, header, face of the bricks to carry the curve round into Station Road. The house was probably built by Thomas Ginn and was intended to continue his Bank Buildings development along Meadow Lane.

35

Chapter 7 STATION ROAD – *east side*

Station Road contains a fascinating array of Victorian warehouses, shops, offices and domestic dwellings. A continuation of its present exclusion from the Sudbury Conservation Area really cannot be justified!

Warehouses
(belonging to 38 Market Hill)

Various factors combine to make these buildings visually interesting; the many variations in the shade of red brick, the subtle changes in direction of the walls and the pair of small semi-circular windows. The left hand section of the warehouses dates from about 1874 when Alfred Halls, "grocer, ale and porter agent" bought 38 Market Hill, then a private property. The range on the right was already there and seems to have been a stable, built around 1840. Note the faded lettering on the wall - "Whitbreads(?) Bottled Ale and Stout" – which probably dates from the years when Holland and Barrett owned these premises.

Kingdom Hall, Station Road

This was once the town Post Office, built in 1911-1912. The architect was Alfred Howard LRIBA. He owned a building and contracting business in Cornard Road before moving to London in 1907 to establish his architectural practice. Clearly he was a very competent architect. The use of a vibrant red brick for the sills, lintels and corner quoins provides visual interest, contrasting with the gleaming white stone and the rather drab brown brick used elsewhere. This may be the first important brick building in the town to use "imported" rather than local bricks - the brownish brick is probably from the London area, brought in by rail.

STATION ROAD – *east side*

Oak Lodge

Oak Lodge and Bank Buildings were clearly designed as a single unit and form an attractive element in the townscape. They date from around 1835; the tall rather narrow sash windows and deep eaves are typical of this time. The fluted doorcase of the Lodge has a simple dignity. The builder was Thomas Ginn and he intended these houses to command fine views across meadowland to the river. Then the railway arrived and the view was of warehouses and sidings! Charles Sillitoe, Teacher of Music, was residing at the Lodge in 1908.

BANK BUILDINGS – *north side*

2-8 Bank Buildings

The whole terrace is included for group value. On the left are Nos 2 and 3, their entrances bracketed beneath a single plain lintel. No 3 was once the Baptist manse and the blue plaque commemorates the Victorian missionary to the Congo, Holman Bentley, who was born there. It once had shutters - note the darker patches on the brickwork and the surviving iron catches. No 5 (the Dental Surgery beyond the gap) incorporates a two storey, timber framed, peg tiled house at the rear, probably early 17thC. Trade Directories record Mrs Catherine Dartnell running a Ladies School at No 6 in 1879 and Making and Cross manufacturing coconut mats at No 7 in 1908.

STATION ROAD – east side

10 Station Road

This striking commercial property has just been refurbished. The red pantiles are a pleasing feature as is the spectacular curved brick corner with moulded brick corbelling above. The windows on the ground floor are modern replacements but reproduce the pattern of the Victorian glazing bars and, crucially, are still recessed the width of a brick - thus helping to maintain the visual integrity of the building. This was William Hitchcock's timber and coal office/ depot, built about 1860. The family business continued here into the 1950's. Behind the building, in Francis Road, you can still see the railway siding that served both the depot and Cundy's seed warehouse.

The document above is one of Hitchcock's invoices, sent in 1895 to the Borough Corporation. He was quoting for the supply of coal to the steam pumping engine at the Waterworks in Woodhall Road. This was quite a journey for the horses which had to pull the waggon from here, through the town, onto Melford Road and then up the steep hill to the engine house. See P86 for further information on the Waterworks.

STATION ROAD – east side

11 Station Road
William Hitchcock lived here next to his business. This is a solid, well proportioned mid-Victorian house, largely in original condition, with no plastic replacement windows or sand blasted brickwork. The front door is excellent, retaining its original stained glass, letterbox and knocker. A change of ownership and all this could be lost.

STATION ROAD – *east side*

The Great Eastern, public house
This photo was taken before the recent facelift, which involved the installation of plastic replacement windows. However the building remains an important Victorian landmark on this busy corner and merits inclusion. The long parapet conceals the sloping roof and just visible on the corner is the inscription "Great Eastern Hotel." Whites Directory 1874 lists Robert Kirby "victualler and horse letter" as managing the business. His initials can still be seen, picked out in white brick against the red, at the side of the building.

14-15 Station Road
Very few terrace properties in this road retain their original windows. However it is sometimes difficult to work out what is original. If this terrace dates from the 1860's then the small panes of No 14 are probably original whilst the larger panes of No 15 may well date from later in the 19th century. The smaller panes give a better rhythm to the facade.

40

STATION ROAD – *west side*

36-38 Station Road

These buildings have recently been acquired by Waitrose and we hope that they will be retained in the redevelopment of the site. No 36 (in the foreground with the blue paint) was the Railway Bell public house. It dates from c1860 and seems to have ceased trading during WW1. The building beyond was the former offices of Barton and Co. which became Bruntons Propellers. These offices were built in 1905. Although some of the windows at the north end were subsequently altered, the fine moulded brickwork of the doorway survives. Outside the former public house on the pavement is an iron cellar grille which still carries the Barton name.

STATION ROAD – detour into EDGWORTH ROAD

STATION ROAD – west side

1-2 Edgworth Road
Stour Valley Villas

Built in 1875 the Villas are interesting both visually and historically. The villas retain their original slate roof. Cast iron was used for the lintels above the windows and for the decorative railings along the window sills. The use of cast iron is not really surprising because the villas were built and occupied by the two men running the iron works across the road. In 1881 Mainprice Barton "engineer employing 18 men and 5 boys" lived in No 1 and Walter Stern "master millwright and engineer" at No 2.

3 Edgworth Road
Primrose Cottage

Although built in 1890, 15 years later, this attractive little cottage shares the same features as its neighbours - the iron works must have retained the original moulds! However a new feature was the casting of the cottage's name into the lintel above the front door. In 1900 Mrs Sarah King, the widow of a former police officer, lived here and was offering "comfortable apartments for single gentlewomen".

39-40 Station Road

An attractive, contrasting pair of semi-detached villas. No 40 has the original brickwork still visible; the use of white brick for the window jambs adds visual interest. On No 39 the original brickwork has been rendered over, giving more of a Georgian feel to the building. Look for an arched window facing Edgworth Road.

outside No 43

Victorian cast iron drain grating (in the gutter), much worn and now adorned with yellow lines but clearly made at Barton's Ironworks. Inscription "Barton & Co Sudbury Suffolk".

STATION ROAD – west side

50 Station Road
An exceptional Victorian shop front. The carving on the brackets is particularly lively. This shop facade may well date back to 1874 when Jacob Jay established his plumbing and decorating business here but the building appears somewhat older. The door on the right led to his "lead and glass warehouse".

JACOB JAY,

HOUSE DECORATOR, PLUMBER AND SANITARY ENGINEER,

50, Station Road, SUDBURY.

Estimates given for General Repairs.

LEAD, GLASS, OIL, AND COLOR WAREHOUSE

STATION ROAD – west side

51 Station Road
Another well proportioned and dignified mid-Victorian frontage with a particularly fine front door with a plain fanlight and keystoned arch above. The double door on the left gives access to a yard behind. Stephen Webb, lime merchant, operated his business both from here and Chilton Road in 1879.

52 Station Road
Another well preserved Victorian shop front with some particularly extravagant carving to the supporting brackets. The shop was built in 1867 and the shopfront could well date from then. In 1874 Miss Fanny Rolfe ran a Christian Knowledge Association depot from here.

53 Station Road (not illustrated)
This adjacent building is included for group value, forming part of one Victorian development with Nos 52 and 54-55. Until recently a music shop, it has been extensively renovated. However it proved impossible to remove all traces of paint from the Ballingdon white bricks.

44

STATION ROAD – *west side*

54-55 Station Road

Only the totally unobservant could fail to notice that this building was erected in 1867 to house the offices and presses of the Suffolk and Essex Free Press. It proclaims its identity with pride! The detailing of the brickwork is still crisp, showing the hardwearing qualities of Ballingdon whites. The heads of the windows are an interesting shape, not quite a curve or a point. Note the Editor's letterbox on the right of the facade. These offices formed one development with the two buildings to the left - Nos 52 and 53. Note how the same decoration continues along the front of all three buildings.

57-59 Station Road

The use of red brick suggests that this row of town houses is Edwardian (early 20thC) but they were erected by the builder Edwin Green at least 30 years earlier - they are referred to in his will of 1883. All were originally built as private dwellings; only No 59 remains as such although strangely, in 1888, it was serving as the Armoury of the Suffolk Regiment 2nd Volunteer Battalion! The front door is original; note the heavy wooden mouldings and fittings. Sadly the Victorian bootscraper was stolen recently. Nos 57 & 58 have intrusive 20thC shop fronts inserted at the ground floor level, but overall this remains an impressive terrace.

CHAPTER 8 - GREAT EASTERN ROAD, CORNARD & NEWTON ROAD

GREAT EASTERN ROAD – north side

Weighbridge
This probably dates from the late 19thC and lies in front of the Carpet Warehouse (formerly a maltings). Two railway sidings came across Great Eastern Road, one on each side of the weighbridge, and goods such as coal could be unloaded directly into waiting waggons. We wonder if any local people can remember it in operation?

CORNARD ROAD – west side

1-6 Cornard Road
The numbering here seems somewhat bizarre. The four houses make an attractive little group, despite modern re-roofing. On the right is the old weatherboarded smithy, converted into a dwelling but carrying no number. Then come a pair of mid 19thC cottages (numbered 2 and 3) and finally No 6 on the left, a more substantial early 19thC house in white brick beneath wide eaves. The 10 pane sashes are unusual and the Georgian doorway with pediment, fanlight and fluted door jambs adds visual interest.

Nettas Dry Cleaners, Great Eastern Road
This building may have a postal address but we have not discovered it ! This is one of the few surviving local buildings directly associated with the Railway Age. It was built in 1895 for Messrs. R.A.Allen and Son who were major brick makers in Ballingdon but also owned various maltings and dealt in coal and lime. Their General Office was downstairs; in the corner you can still see the original walk-in safe with massive iron door. The exterior has been little altered over the years apart from some lowering of window sills on the ground floor. On the corner there is a pleasing curved brick wall with moulded brick corbelling above. This should be preserved as an excellent local example of a late Victorian commercial office.

CORNARD ROAD – west side

CORNARD ROAD – east side

Stephen Walters Mill
Very plain yet demonstrating that a functional building can still be attractive. This building is also historically important because it was the first power driven silk mill to open in Sudbury. It was built c1890 by Kipling, Dennler and Company. Stephen Walters took it over in about 1896 when Kipling Dennler became insolvent; the firm still makes silk here today.

22-24 Cornard Road
Of both visual and local historic interest - all that is left today of Oliver's Brewery. On the left are their offices, extensively rebuilt in 1902. The architect was A.A.Hunt. White brick is used for the detailing and, at the far end of the building on the south side, there is a fine oriel window from where the Oliver brothers could keep an eye on their workmen in the yard below. The doorway at the south end of the building, athough now blocked, is another good feature. On the right there stands Brewery House where the 1891 Census listed Edward Oliver, brewer, his wife Emily, their 5 children and 2 servants. The front door, with its stained glass fanlight, is original.

55 Cornard Road
Justin House was built in 1864 and is a most individual and striking building. The two gables are of unequal width and the right hand gable alone is half hipped and has a carved bargeboard. The fishscale tiles on the roof add to the interest; they seem to belong to Kent or Sussex rather than East Anglia. The windows add the finishing touch. The pointed sash windows, set in pairs beneath shallow pointed lintels, have no parallel elsewhere in the town - their style has been called "vernacular ecclesiastical" by one writer.

47

CORNARD ROAD – *east side*

Ardmore, 57 Cornard Road
In contrast to No 55, Ardmore reflects a foreign influence - that of Renaissance Italy. The entrance tower, with its circular windows and deep overhanging eaves, dominates the whole building and has the feel of Tuscany. There are interesting differences in style between the arches above the ground floor windows and those on the first floor, all adding to the visual interest of the building. It has served as the local veterinary surgery for many years.

BELLE VUE ROAD – *west side*

13 Belle Vue Road, Homeland
This Edwardian house was built in 1912 by Frederick Wheeler, the East Street grazier and butcher, on land which was formerly part of the grounds of East House. It has remained in his family ever since. He had built up a collection of second hand doors, windows and other materials and seems to have given a local builder the task of incorporating them into a house! The result works surprisingly well. The ironwork of the long verandah which spans the facade of the house is particularly attractive and the door knocker and letterbox are also good original features.

NEWTON ROAD – north side

7 Newton Road, Chelsea Lodge

Chelsea Lodge would not look out of place to the north of Bury or up on the Breckland where this combination of flint cobbles and white brick is more common than in Sudbury. It was probably built about 1840 and still retains the original front door, gate and railings even if a large conservatory and separate bakehouse have long gone. An harmonious building with the shutters adding to the visual interest.

Sudbury Cemetery

When the town cemetery was opened in 1859 these twin chapels were built, one for Nonconformist and the other for Anglican services. However at least the two religious groups could agree on the overall style of the chapels - Gothic revival "Decorated." They were built combining traditional flint with local white brick for most of the detailing.

Cemetery gates and walls

The original iron gates, mounted on white brick pillars with stone caps, survive intact as do the walls around the Cemetery. These gates were presumably made locally. A close study of the locks on the two gates reveals that they were made by different local ironsmiths, Purr and C. Wright. Perhaps the contract was shared out to keep both of them happy.

49

NEWTON ROAD – *south side*

Belle Vue

The first Belle Vue was pulled down in 1871 and this mansion erected in its place by Edmund Stedman, the Town Clerk. Judging by old prints its predecessor was far more elegant and restrained. This photo shows what is definitely the more attractive side of the present building; the north side is marred by an ornate and grandiose porch. Belle Vue served as Sudbury Borough Council offices from about 1918 to 1974 and is still serving the community as an Adult Education Centre.

Ventnor and Oakdene

These imposing villas, built in the early 1870's, have a restrained but expensive elegance - note how white brick is used for all the elevations (not just the fronts) and all the arched door and window lintels are of carefully fitted gauged (tapered) bricks. Above the deep eaves the chimneys stand tall and proud like the funnels of an ocean liner. We know that Francis Mayland Francis, a prominent local corn merchant and maltster, was an early resident here but we are unsure about which villa he occupied.

CHAPTER 9 - EAST STREET & WALDINGFIELD ROAD

EAST STREET – north side

White Horse Stables
This stable range lies in a yard opposite Somerfield Supermarket. The long unbroken span of the peg tiled roof is particularly attractive. Many local inns still retain their stables from the days when coach operators, carriers and farmers coming to market needed stabling facilities. Many inn keepers also hired out horses. Hay and feed for the horses was stored on the first floor. To the right of the stables is the side of the Queensbury building.

2 East Street, Queensbury
This well known landmark stands at the corner of East and Girling Streets. It began its life c1880 as a three storey maltings owned by Joseph Stammers Garrett. In 1919 it was converted into Melso's textile mill and then, in 1945, into Cundy's seed store. The old photo c1950 shows a group of Cundy's workers loading bagged seed. It also reveals that the maltings was built in red brick with white brick banding, although all the brickwork is now covered in white paint. The right hand section was recently demolished in the course of work to give these old buildings yet another lease of life as flats and a public house.

51

EAST STREET – north side

12-14 East Street
The black paint on No 14 (Ali's Toy Shed) makes it difficult to see but the Victorian fascia actually continues across both shops. Indeed in 1888 James Nightingale, a cabinet maker, occupied the whole range. Well into the 20thC both sides of East Street were lined with shops, supplying most of the everyday needs of local people.

7-8 East Street
The steeply pitched and peg tiled roof suggests that this was once a single timber framed building, probably 17thC in date, which was subsequently divided into two properties. A Victorian brick front was then added to No 7 together with a decorated string course composed of cable and floral motifs. No 8 (Chapel Belles) was left with its original lath and plaster walls. The result is interesting but something of a visual hotchpotch! The two shop fronts are probably late 19th/early 20thC. In 1908 Oscar Unwin, a baker, was at No 7 and Jesse Green, fishmonger, at No 8.

20 East Street
Here is another shop which still retains its Victorian fascia more or less intact although clearly in need of some refurbishment. Elijah Scott ran a grocery business here in 1908. However, the building itself is probably 17thC. The steep pitch of the roof was intended for thatch or tiles, not slate, and there is still some internal exposed timberwork, as indeed there is in the property to the left.

52

EAST STREET – north side

29 East Street
A late 19thC white painted brick cottage featuring a large shop window divided into six panes with, on the left, the original front door set beneath a plain fanlight. Three simple pilasters frame both shop window and door and various hooks and fittings indicate that the shop window once had a projecting blind. Some local people still remember it as a baker's shop. George Gilder was the baker here in 1908.

Horse & Groom, Public House
A substantial late Victorian pub c1885 with all its original sash windows. The "cutaway" on the corner is both decorative and practical, giving some protection from collision with turning waggons. There is also this attractive range of pantiled stables and outhouses in the pub yard off Upper East Street.

EAST STREET – north side

EAST STREET – south side

88-89 East Street
The warm red brick suggest a late 18th/early19thC house but it seems to be a later refronting of an older building. The double doors on the left led to the former smithy which projects behind the main property. In 1908 the blacksmith was Frederick Kemp. The present shoe shop has been a family business since the 1920's and the insertion of a shop window may well date from that time.

Eastgate House
This substantial double fronted property dominates the junction of East Street and Upper East Street. The bay windows flanking the entrance are carried up through both floors, giving a feeling of great balance to the building. The decoration is quite subdued, just a cable motif for the string course and a floral pattern on the window lintels and door arch. It probably dates from about 1880.

48-51 East Street
The three storey weavers' cottages on the right are listed. This two storey row was originally three storey but was reduced in height following bomb damage suffered during the German Zeppelin raid on Sudbury in 1916. However, they retain the wide windows on the first floor which gave the weaver maximum light to work on his hand loom.

WALDINGFIELD ROAD – north side

In the late 19thC the town began to expand significantly along the approach roads to the east and north. These properties have been chosen as good examples of the middle class villas built at that time...

1-3 East Street, Laburnham Villas 1881

An attractive pair of well proportioned semi-detached houses built by Wheeler and Son of 89 East Street. All the walls are of white brick, always a good indicator of quality - often cheaper red brick was used at the back and sides. Brick pilasters stand at each corner; the front doors are recessed within a shared porch and are flanked by ground floor bay windows. The detailing is restrained - some moulded brick detailing above the porch and a line of bricks set at 45 degrees beneath the eaves.

19 Waldingfield Road, Rose Villa 1878

Rose Villa stands on land once known as Pigtail Piece - perhaps this explains the high fertility of the soil here! In 1878 the plot was bought for £50 by Joseph Barwick, a solicitor's clerk. He then borrowed £230 from Robert Ransom, solicitor, to have the house built but subsequently lost the property when Ransom foreclosed on him. The projecting two storey bay is an attractive feature; note how the brickwork is chamfered on each side of the sash windows. Both the original wooden porch and door survive, adding to the visual interest of this villa.

35-37 Waldingfield Road, Clifton Villas 1884

Bath stone rather than a cheap cement render is used for all the detailing, including the flower decorated keystones over the doors and the crocketed capitals framing both windows and doors. As a result the carvings are still very crisp and show little sign of weathering. Probably built by Grimwood & Sons.

WALDINGFIELD ROAD – *north side*

43 Waldingfield Road, Albion House 1893

An unusual and imposing design. The porch is carried up to the first floor so that it forms a projecting gabled tower. A double string course of nailhead decoration relieves the severity of the building.

39 Waldingfield Road, Villa Firenze 1880

Both the name and the detailing around the door and windows shows the strong influence that Italian buildings had on some English architects at this time. The Bath stone detailing is very fine - note the Early Gothic crocketed capitals at the top of the corner pilasters and on the door way. It is said that Nos 39 and 41 were built by Arthur Grimwood after he returned, inspired, from a trip to Italy!

WALDINGFIELD ROAD – north side

NEWMANS ROAD – east side

This narrow, steep cul de sac lies opposite Elizabeth Court on the north side of East Street. It contains many interesting Victorian workers' houses, all fronting directly onto the pavement.

18-20 Newmans Road, Surrey Cottages 1888

They make an attractive pair, totally without decorative frills but visually very satisfying. The slate roofs of the individual bay windows join up to form a double porch supported by a single cast iron column. They were probably built by Elliston and Son of Gaol Lane. The 1891 Census groups not two but four cottages together as "Surrey Cottages" with a stone mason, a groom, a joiner and a carpenter in residence. Very confusing, but at least it gives a good idea of the kind of workmen who could afford the rents on these houses.

57 Waldingfield Road,

This villa just fits into a rather narrow building plot; note how close its eaves are to No 55. White brick is used for the front but red brick with white banding at the sides and rear. A square ground floor bay supports a three sided bay on the first floor. The rusticated segmental arches to the first floor windows and the fine detailing of the archway above the recessed front door are noteworthy features. Probably built by C.E.Dennington c1895.

28-34 Newmans Road, Belvedere Cottages 1904

These cottages continue the linked porch theme but dispenses with the supporting column. A central passageway gives access to the rear - a common feature in Victorian terraces of four or more houses. As with Surrey Cottages, all these homes have their original sash windows.

57

CHAPTER 10 - MARKET HILL to GAOL LANE

around MARKET HILL - eastern end   - western end

46 Market Hill, HSBC Bank
Unlike the majority of the buildings around Market Hill the former Midland Bank building of 1920 is unlisted. The name of the architect is not known but clearly the design reflected the "house style" - Head Offices's view on what a bank should look like - and makes no reference to local building traditions. The style is metropolitan and indeed almost Baroque in feel. However the bank has been part of the local townscape for many years and undeniably it makes a strong, confident visual statement, dominating this corner site. Indeed it expanded in both directions in the 1980's to include the neighbouring shops on each side. The copper cupola and the grand entrance with swan necked pediment both catch the eye.

10 Old Market Place
This building makes a very strong visual statement seen from North Street. The architect was F.P.Trepess from Warwick and he designed it in 1908 for Walker and Company, a national chain of grocery and general stores. The soaring gable with leaded light window is a major feature but dominating everything is the extraordinary bank of small paned windows set in iron frames (the latter feature quite innovative for this time).

Water fountain, Market Hill 1882
The fountain was presented to the town by Alice Mary Brown. The metal fountain head has disappeared; but some Sudburians can still remember it working. Presumably the water ran down, first to people, then horses and finally cats and dogs - it famously features in Dodie Smith's book "One Hundred and One Dalmatians" and now carries a plaque to that effect.

GAOL LANE – west side

GROUP OF THREE WAREHOUSES

These three warehouses were built on the west side of the lane by R.S.Joy to serve his furnishing, funeral and removal business. They were later taken over by P.S.Head in 1919. Nos 21 & 21A are in a courtyard reached by a passageway to the left of Toymaster Kingdom. They all have considerable character as well as local historical significance.

21 Gaol Lane (r) "Mill House Warehouse"

An imposing two storey red brick building of c1885 with a single storey lean-to waggon shed and stable at the side. Here Mr Joy kept his horse drawn hearse. The curved wall on the corner had a practical value - it was less likely to be damaged by a waggon. Today we admire the skill of the bricklayer.

21A Gaol Lane (r) "The White Elephant"

This name was given the building during Mr Head's ownership, partly because of its dominant colour and partly because of his difficulty finding a good use for it! The sides of the warehouse facing the internal courtyard of Gaol Lane are in white brick. This photo of the south west elevation was taken from Old Market Court (off Burkitts Lane). Mr Joy's initials, RSJ, and the date, 1903, feature on the plaque, visible above the car. The warehouse is severe in appearance but nevertheless impressive.

23 Gaol Lane (l) "Toymaster Kingdom"

A long, narrow, red brick and slate warehouse built in 1899. The facade with its framing pilasters is original; the doors were wide enough to admit a horse drawn removal van.

GAOL LANE – west side

47-49 Gaol Lane (r)
The visual appeal of these properties is self evident but difficult to quantify. It is partly their balance and proportion, partly their retention of many original features such as doors, fanlights and sash windows. The bricks also have an attractive patina that has built up over the years. We think that they date from the 1840's.

25-39 Gaol Lane
Siam Terrace dates from 1890. Similar terraces of workers' cottages in the town have been much altered by replacement windows and doors but the majority of the houses in this terrace retain their original features. Nos 29 and 31 are illustrated but the whole terrace is sufficiently intact to have a group value.

Siam House garden wall & 3 Siam Place, 1869
Siam House was the Victorian home of the Elliston family who ran a local building firm. The house was pulled down c.1970 but this attractive garden wall survives together with part of the garden it enclosed. The town's old walls are an important part of the townscape; this is a particularly good mid 19thC example. On the right is Terry Cottage, No 3 Siam Place. The cottage has survived almost in its original condition. The iron railings on the window sills are an unusual feature as is the unusual yellow colour of the bricks used. Were these local bricks and why was it named Terry Cottage?

CHAPTER 11 - GAINSBOROUGH STREET to GREGORY STREET

GAINSBOROUGH STREET – south side

2-4 Gainsborough Street

Passers by rarely give this mixed two/three storey range an upward glance. It was purpose built as a small shopping development about 1870. No 1 was absorbed into the Midland Bank in the late 20thC whilst the others still remain as shops. The upper windows are set below attractive decorated lintels with supporting brackets but are all set at slightly different levels. Is this the result of Victorian jerry building or modern traffic vibration? Nos 3 and 4 incorporate an earlier wattle and daub rear wall.

9 Gainsborough Street

An elegant and refined building dating from about 1840. Clearly no money was spared in its construction, particularly in the use of stone for the door case and window lintels. From Christopher Lane, the rear of the building is equally impressive; note the fine brickwork in the curved wall and the carved wooden pelmet above the sash window. Presumably the stable and coach house further down the Lane on the left also belonged to the house.

61

GAINSBOROUGH STREET – south side

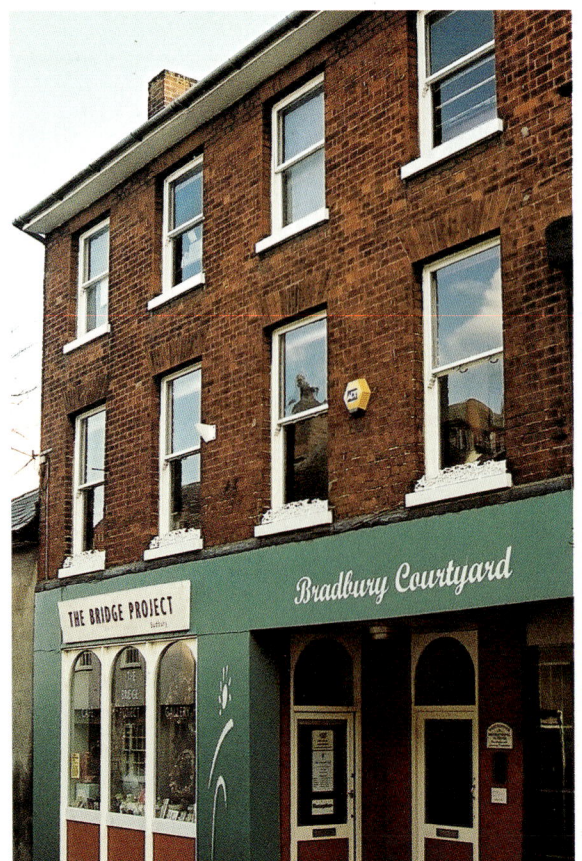

Milestone (outside No.16, Milestone House)
This unobtrusive triangular stone dates from the late18th/early 19thC and was probably erected by a local Turnpike Company. Approaching from Market Hill it reads "56 miles to London"; coming into the town centre it reads "56 miles from London"! The stone needs resetting so that the lower inscription is more visible.

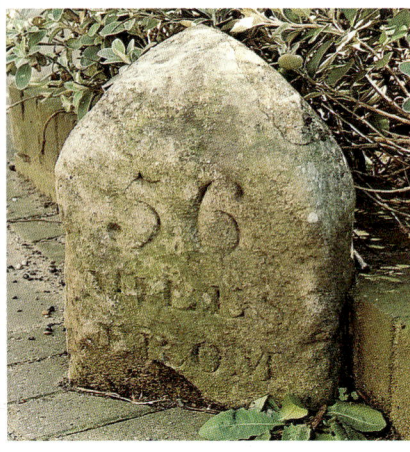

20 Gainsborough Street
This three storey red brick building and entrance way dominates this part of the street. It has been refurbished recently and has an undeniable presence. Edwin Green, builder and contractor, was established at No 20 Sepulchre Street by 1864 and the building may date from his time. However, by 1896 Green had been succeeded here by Eli Cross, builder, contractor and undertaker; we feel it more likely that he built the red brick frontage. Note the attractive two storey pantiled shed in the courtyard behind. The buildings now house The Bridge Project.

– north side

"The Drill Hall" 1881
An impressive and highly original building, very much a one off! The white stone used for the detailing works well against the rich red of the brickwork. The Tudor-style entrance and the large oriel window above dominate the facade. The architect, Arthur Grimwood, clearly loved his gables but had problems finding a way of carrying off rain water without cluttering the facade with drainpipes. His solution was quirky but adds to the interest of the building. His father, George Henry Grimwood laid the foundation stone as Mayor and, as head of the family firm, supervised its construction.

GAINSBOROUGH STREET – north side

50-52 Gainsborough Street

This late Victorian range has changed very little since it appeared in a 1906 advertisement for W.J.Backler's Clothing Stores. However, it has subsequently been broken into two shops. The alternating design of the first floor sash windows is rather odd but adds visual interest, as do the projecting dormer windows above.

48-49 Gainsborough Street

The fine mid Victorian facade of No 48 repays study. The detailing around the arched windows and along the string course is very fine. On the side facing Weavers Lane the brickwork is rendered and then scribed to imitate stone whilst, unusually, the ground floor windows have cast iron lintels. The photo also shows No 49 (on the right) which seems to date from the 1870's although the green and white tilework of the shop front is probably early 20thC. The carving of the woodwork around the oriel window is extremely delicate. In 1874 Jas. Hyde, greengrocer and pork butcher, had his shop here and, in this century, Mr Cook and then Mr Sepping, also butchers.

GREGORY STREET – *east side*

Gregory Mills, 1912
Despite its date this building belongs very much to the Modern Movement, usually taken to date from the 1920's. The pattern of wooden glazing bars has an angular Art Deco look. The architect, A.Howard LRIBA, designed these offices for the Sudbury Silk Weaving Company which became Vanners and Fennell in 1924. Local people have worked in the silk mills behind the Gregory Street frontage for well over 100 years.

The Pentecostal Church, 1863
This was built as a Primitive Methodist Church. The style is classical with a dominating broken pediment and a well balanced arrangement of door and round arched windows. The moulded brick detailing is restrained; note the touch of red brick up in the gable. There is a feeling of serenity about this building.

CHAPTER 12 - THE CROFT & CHURCH WALK

THE CROFT – south east side, Nos 1-5

This attractive group of houses lies on the edge of the Croft. Cars are usually parked along the narrow road but the large photo shows the view without vehicles, allowing us to appreciate the simple attractions of these buildings, all faced in local white brick but with considerable variations in height, width and roof pitch. They have a group value but particular buildings are selected for comment.

LOT 1.
THE WELL-BUILT AND CONVENIENTLY PLACED
DWELLING HOUSE
AND
Manufacturing Premises,
OF WHITE BRICK & SLATE CONSTRUCTION,
Situate and being No. 1, The Croft, with a return frontage of 104ft. to Croft Road.

The DWELLING HOUSE, which has a pleasant frontage to the Croft, CONTAINS

IN THE BASEMENT—Good Cellarage.
ON THE GROUND FLOOR—Entrance Passage, Front Parlour 15ft. × 13ft., fitted with Two Cupboards, Keeping Room 14ft. × 10ft., Kitchen with Cupboards and a well-fitted Dresser.
ON THE FIRST FLOOR—Landing with Cupboards and Three Good Bedrooms with Stoves, the two principal rooms being 17ft. 6in. × 15ft. 6in., and 16ft. × 10ft.

THE FACTORY COMPRISES
Two Well-lighted Floors, each about 30ft. × 16ft., Entrance Lobby from Croft Road, and a Room suitable for Office. There is a Paved Yard at side with Glazed Roof and an
OPEN YARD with a frontage of 36ft. by a depth of 49ft. (available as Building Site), with close-boarded Folding Gates towards Croft Road.
WATER AND GAS ARE LAID ON.

A right-of-way to the road is reserved for Lots 2, 3 and 4, as shown on Plan, which will be produced at the time of Sale.

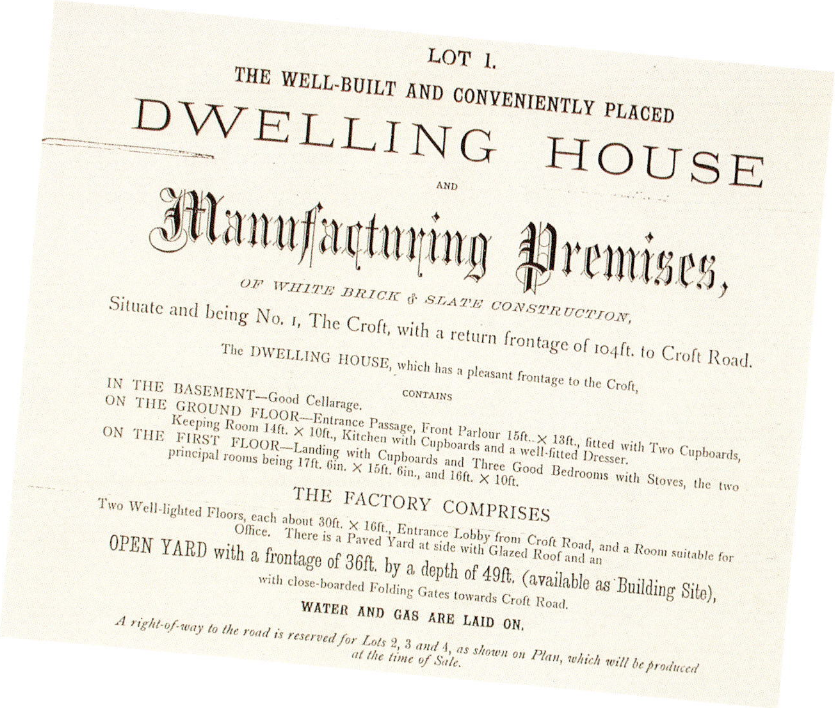

1 The Croft, Northcroft Social Club

The photo shows the return frontage to Croft Road. No 1 began as a mid-Victorian private house on the Croft. By 1873 Charles Wright, crayon manufacturer, was living in the house and had built this factory behind, facing onto Croft Road. The auction notice of October 26th 1897 refers to both the private house and the factory. In the 20thC these premises successively housed the Liberal Club and the British Legion. A rather bleak looking building but it is of local historical interest.

65

THE CROFT – south east side

4 The Croft
A great contrast to its neighbours. The narrow frontage and steeply pitched peg tiled roof indicate a survival from a much earlier period. The Victorian brick facade with contemporary sashes protrudes slightly in front of the building line of neighbouring houses, indicating that it was added to an earlier timber framed building.

2 The Croft (l)
A well proportioned double fronted mid 19thC house with original sashes set below cambered brick lintels. The shallow pitch of the roof is characteristic of Victorian house roofs built for slating rather than tiling.

5 The Croft, St Annes (r)
A dignified, well proportioned early 19thC house with simple rubbed brick doorway arch and fanlight below. The upper floor sashes are original but the lower sashes are late 19thC, possibly inserted to allow more light into the front rooms. In the early 20thC this was the family home of Charles George Grimwood, lessee of the Quay Lane Gas Works. No 5 is believed to stand on the site of the ancient "pie powder" court and gaol which sought to deal with disorderly behaviour and sharp practice at the annual fairs on The Croft. These were discontinued in 1862 "since they had deteriorated into mere pleasure fairs to the hindrance of the trade of the town".

THE CROFT – north east side

North House and 28 The Croft

A very impressive pair of houses c1880 which dominate the high ground on this corner site. The wooden porches are restrained and classical in feel; brick pilasters are grouped with great skill at the centre and corners to give rhythm to the whole building. Together the two houses are more than the sum total of their parts, almost a mansion in appearance.

Drain Grating (adjacent to the Convent)

This may be found about 12 feet to the right of the pedestrian entrance to the Convent. Generations of Sudburians have walked over this cast iron grating, wearing away the lettering. It reads "W.I.Green Sudbury". One other local example has been found; they are the only surviving evidence of this firm's existence in the town apart from listings in late Victorian trade directories and the odd surviving invoice. Kelly's 1888 Directory records Green as "a brass and iron founder" in Birketts Lane. The site is now occupied by the used car saleroom at the rear of the Oxfam shop.

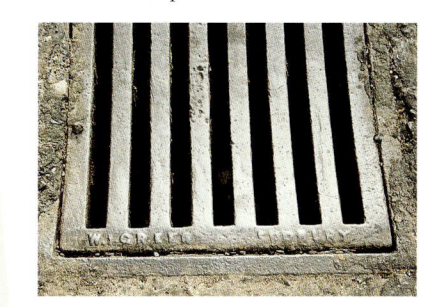

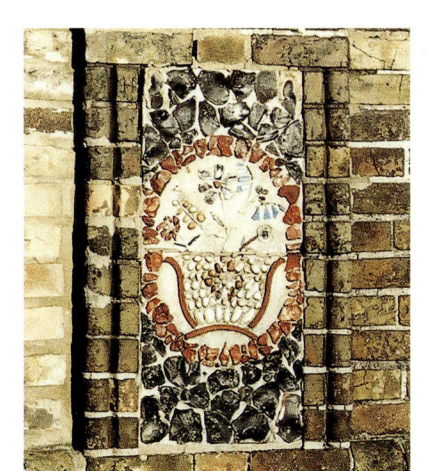

Mosaic wall to Croft Cottage

A series of five mosaic panels set within frames of moulded brick, all rather naive, but contributing to the variety and interest of the local scene. Oral tradition says that they were made in the late 19thC by the elderly man who lived there and that, along with his dog, he later died in a fire in the house

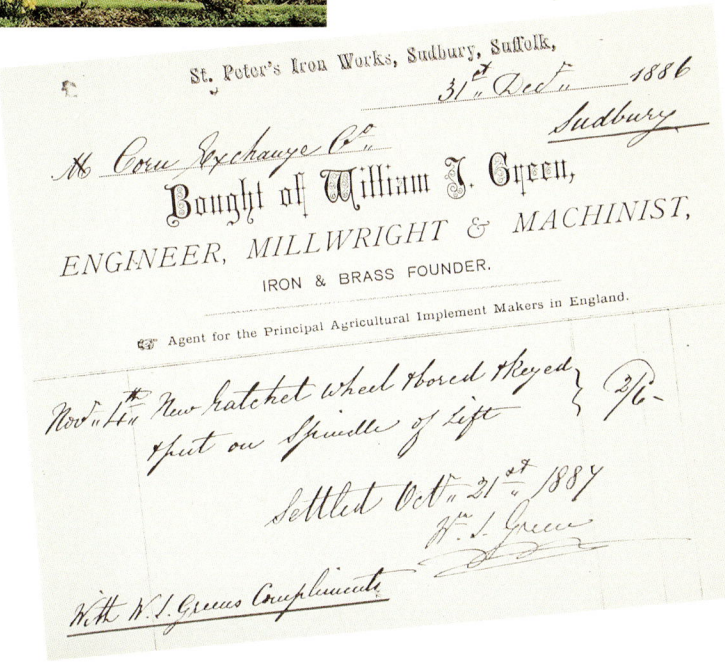

67

CHURCH WALK – *west side*

1 Church Walk
This house actually sits on the west side of Acton Square. It is by any standards a highly idiosyncratic building but one which adds interest and colour to the townscape, not least for the alien blow up dolls which can be seen in its windows! It was built c1891 to serve as the offices of Grimwood's building firm and their other interests such as the Cornard Brick Company. It features an extraordinary mix of different design elements and building materials. This was probably quite deliberate, demonstrating the firm's building talents to prospective customers. The firm's architect, Arthur Grimwood had his drawing office here.

2-4 Church Walk
Shown above this appears to be a row of three mid Victorian cottages but the steep pitch of the peg tiled roof and the internal studwork and lath and plaster walls indicate an older building (early 18thC?) with a white brick facade added subsequently in the 19thC.

6 Church Walk
This attractive small timber framed cottage stands across the road from the Waggon and Horses. The mansard roof is not a very common type in the town; it gave extra space and more headroom on the first floor than a conventional pitched roof but was more expensive to construct. Probably 17thC in origin.

68

CHURCH WALK – east side

The 1902 photograph shows Harriet on the right, her son, Charles William Grimwood on the left, and his son Charles George in the centre. Both in turn managed the town Gas Works. The child in the centre is Kathleen Grimwood, now 101 years old. Her twin sister Gertrude is on the left.

Waggon & Horses, Public House

The pub dates back at least as far as 1844 when Shadrach Clover was the innkeeper. However, the peg tiled house which is at the heart of the pub may well be 18thC. The double doorway and surrounding small window panes in the slate roofed section have a Dickensian feel and are the best features of a pub that is not short of character. There is also a good range of stables and outbuildings on the side facing Croft Road. George Grimwood, the founder of the building firm, was also the innkeeper but after his death his widow, Harriet, ran it for many years. The small offices on the extreme left of the main photo marked the entrance to their Phoenix Brewery.

Wall & plaque 1890

Grimwood's builder's yard lay behind this wall. It contained a large two storey building with workshops and offices above and timber and stored materials below. When the fire broke out about 40 men were on the premises; those in the joiner's shop had to jump for their lives. After the fire the yard was relocated to Weavers Lane (where Weavers Court is now) and the Grimwoods built The Phoenix Brewery on this site, literally rising out of the ashes.

69

Chapter 13 AROUND ACTON SQUARE

This section looks at buildings in Acton Square and in three of the four roads which radiate from it (Church Walk was covered in the previous chapter). We have used the name Acton Square but its correct name is Acton Green.

WEAVERS LANE – west side

This fine example of the iron founder's art can be found between No 2 and the Print Workshop. In many ways Sudbury in the late 19thC was an extremely self sufficient community and many needs could be supplied locally. Thus the town had a number of local iron foundries and the evidence still exists in the large number of old iron gates and railings around the town which somehow escaped the drive for scrap in WW2.

9-12 Burkitts Lane

Illustrated here are three rendered brick Victorian cottages, c1880. They are well proportioned and have retained original features such as their sash windows and boot scrapers. The pastel shades chosen for the rendering are hardly traditional Suffolk colours but introduce a bright seaside feel to this part of the lane. No 12 (not illustrated) is a more substantial double fronted Victorian property, also rendered, with original sashes on the ground floor but replacement wooden casements above. Window shutters give the house added visual interest but are probably a later addition from the early 20thC, the result of greater contact with the Continent. The four houses have a group value within the local townscape.

BURKITTS LANE – west side

– east side

Stables of Black Boy public house

These pantiled stables lie at the rear of the old coaching inn on Market Hill. They are timber framed with a mixture of brick and weather boarding used for the walls. Inside the floor is of well worn white brick, much sunken at the entrance where the heavy horses came in. The original stalls for the horses survive intact. The hay loft above was once used as a store by the Sudbury Dramatic Society before their move to The Quay in the 1970's. The range probably dates from the mid 19thC. A simple, functional building which adds variety and interest to the townscape.

BURKITTS LANE – *east side*

21-22 Burkitts Lane

An attractive pair of mid 19thC houses with the basements at pavement level, giving them quite a sophisticated metropolitan feel. The semi-circular brick door arches surround simple fanlights, each with a single vertical glazing bar. Note how the brickwork around the doors and windows is chamfered whilst the window lintels are of cast iron - they could well have come from William Green's ironworks just along the Lane and he may also have supplied the decorative railings. We tend not to look at chimney pots but these are worth an upward look. Note also, on the chimney, how protruding bricks are used to protect the edges of the lead flashing around the chimney from driving rain; all good details, indicative of a building of quality. Views differ on the merits of cleaning walls made of Ballingdon whites - we prefer the natural patina built up over the years.

ACTON SQUARE — north side

The Square contains an interesting variety of buildings from different periods including some striking modern houses such as No 2. This process continues; currently the site of Acton Square Buildings Supplies on the south side is awaiting redevelopment for housing.

3-6 Acton Square

This mid Victorian terrace has a simple dignity. We suspect that the sashes are modern replacements from when the cottages were refurbished but they preserve the original appearance of the terrace. No 3 (on the extreme left) has a large ground floor window space from when it was once a butcher's shop. Note the brickwork on the extreme right, resembling the section of a Norman column. A curved corner like this was less vulnerable to damage from heavy waggons than a conventional 90 degree corner. The adjacent blue street sign gives the correct name, not a Square but a Green. Sadly cars have long replaced the grass!

— east side

8-10 Acton Square

An unusually short terrace of just three houses. Of the three, Nos 8 and 10 retain their original windows although the pipework on No 8 must surely be a later modification! All the brick detailing is very crisp - note the copying of Norman motifs on the string course (nail head and cable), the moulded bricks making up the window and doorway lintels and the stepped corbelling on the corner.

ACTON SQUARE – east side

'The Dental Emporium' 11 Acton Square

These buildings have considerable visual and historical importance. They date from c1870 and were built by the firm of Stephen Walters as its first base in the town (note the "W" high up in the north west gable). Subsequently both Vanners and Gainsborough Silk Co. occupied the factory, so all three of the surviving silk firms in Sudbury have been based here at one time or other. The early photo c1900 appear to show power driven winding machines on the upper floor; at that time most weaving was still being carried out by handloom weavers in their own cottages. The use of red brick for contrast against the predominant white is a noticeable feature; this practice became popular in England after John Ruskin published his book "Stones of Venice" in 1851. The manager or foreman's house at the side has retained more of its original appearance than the factory which now has modern sealed unit replacement windows. However glazing bars have now been fitted, restoring something of the "feel" of a 19thC silk mill.

CROFT ROAD – *east side*

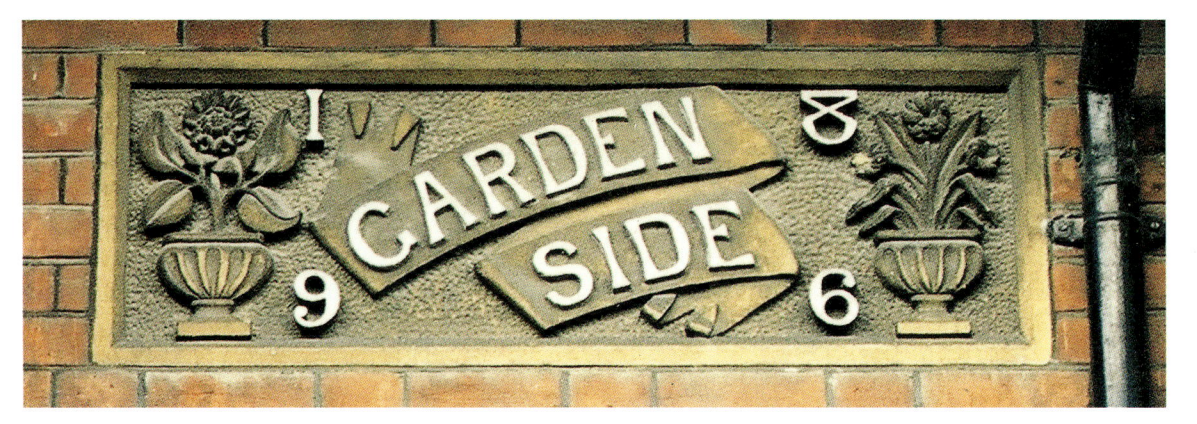

Chapter 14
NEW STREET & PRINCE STREET

1-4 'Gardenside' 1896

Many architects in the late 19thC were looking again at traditional English vernacular architecture and using features such as these half timbered, tile hung gables. The terrace was built by George Grimwood and Sons whose office and yard were literally only a few yards away. The actual design work would have been carried out by the architect of the family firm, Arthur Grimwood, from his office in No 1 Church Walk. In his case perhaps the old merchants' houses in Stour Street were a source of inspiration. The name plaque is particularly fine; the depth of the floral designs suggests that it is a genuine carving in stone rather than a cheaper moulding.

NEW STREET - *south side*

1-6 New Street

A fine row of weavers' cottages c1860. They appear a cut above other such terraces in the town. The white brickwork is very good quality and the red brick lintels provide a pleasing contrast. The central raised parapet suggests that the terrace may once have carried a name. No 5 (second from right) is of particular interest because it still has its original small paned windows as well as its slate roof. Edward Bonney was working at his loom here in 1881; the extra wide first floor window helped to give him maximum light. In 1900 a firm of umbrella silk manufacturers, Kipling and Company, was based at No 1. It probably operated as a depot for supplying "thrown" silk to local handloom weavers.

NEW STREET – south side

Grace Baptist Church 1858

Founded by the Grace or Ebenezer Baptists this simple, unadorned chapel contrasts dramatically with the imposing Baptist church erected in Church Street (from which they had broken away). Even the use of lower status red brick may have been a deliberate choice to emphasise the simplicity of their beliefs and services; of course red brick was also softer and therefore cheaper than white. Here white is reserved for the detailing - round doors, windows and at the corners. Crowds of up to 2000 people would gather on The Croft to witness them baptising new members in the River Stour.

7 New Street

Included for its simple Victorian shop front in the ground floor bay. Henry Smith, boot and shoemaker, was living here in 1881 with his unmarried son Angelo Smith, watch and clock maker. Angelo was the founder of the long established family business which is still located at No 4 North Street.

10-11 New Street

This pair of simple yet well proportioned cottages retain their original mid-Victorian sash windows. Too often modern plastic windows are fitted which fail to reproduce the original glazing pattern, affecting not just the property itself but the appearance of the whole terrace. In 1881 Joseph Amos, silk weaver, lived at No 10 and William Griggs, postman and boot maker, at No 11.

NEW STREET – south side   – north side

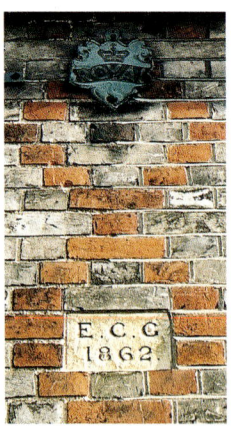

21-23 New Street
(with 26-28 - not illustrated)
Nos 21-23 and Nos 26-28 have been picked out because they still retain their original sash windows. This long terrace of attractive cottages ascends the rising ground with the red brick detailing helping to lead the eye up the hill from one group to another. There is no datestone but we feel that they probably date from the 1860's when the Street was really "New". The tall but rather narrow sash windows give an impression of height and the cottages have a simple dignity. In 1881 Nos 21-23 were occupied respectively by a laundress, a tailor and a wheelwright. The satellite dishes are intrusive but seem an inescapable fact of modern life.

15-18 New Street, Lentons Terrace 1862
These four cottages at the western end of the street are surprisingly ornate. The builder was Edwin Coote Green. Note the use of both red and overfired black bricks to provide a decorative string course and diaper patterns on the chimneys and wall. The wedge shaped window lintels are unusual for Sudbury. Note the "Royal" insurance firemark above the datestone and, out of the photo, the name of the terrace, insignificant and easy to miss. Plenty of visual interest in these cottages!

NEW STREET – north side

Former Steam Mill, New Street

An impressive three storey, brick built mill c1865 with a loading door on the first floor and an overhanging hoist up in the attic above. The steam engine may have been housed in the lean-to structure at the side. Note that the window lintels are of cast iron. John Wilson, miller and baker, was in business here in 1868 - his shop still stands on the corner with North Street. Many older Sudburians remember the shop as Oakley's Bakers and the road below the hoist being often dusted with flour. At the rear of the shop by the lamp post is a fine example of the skill of local bricklayers.

NEW STREET – north side

New Hall, New Street

This long, single storey factory, built of brick, timber and slate, is situated in a yard off New Street. However, when the yard gates are closed it is still visible from the Melford Road. We think of the long banks of small paned windows as an attractive period feature but of course they were originally purely functional - to let as much light in as possible for stay making. It was purpose-built by Thomas Holland, a local builder, probably soon after he acquired the site in 1863. It was then occupied in turn by three stay making firms, the last being William Pretty of Ipswich. The factory fell victim to the Great Depression and changing female fashions and in 1930 it was purchased by The Conservative Club and became a skittle alley. In 1944 CAV moved here from West London to establish their first presence in the town so the building is of both visual and local historical importance.

GAINSBOROUGH ROAD – north side

8-10 Gainsborough Road

This elegant pair of late Edwardian villas faces down Prince Street. No10 on the right has been recently restored with great care and sensitivity. Both properties have the bay windows characteristic of the late 19th/early 20thC. Such windows helped to bring more light into front rooms and also helped residents to keep an eye on the coming and going of neighbours! On these bays the detail of the woodwork is particularly good; the crisp moulded brickwork above the first floor windows is an interesting feature, based on the Norman beakhead design. We believe that the villas were designed by the local artist, architect and teacher, F.P.Earee.

PRINCE STREET - east side

11-18 Girton Terrace 1884

In 1884 this terrace must have been a model of elegance and restrained good taste; the quality of the stone lintels is particularly fine. When the local firm of Grimwood and Sons secured the contract to build Girton College in Cambridge, there was a row of cottages on site which had to be demolished. The stonework was saved and reused here in Sudbury. This was easy to do in those days when there was still a direct rail link. The unity of the terrace has been disturbed by the painting of the brickwork on two houses and by many modern replacement windows including some where glazing bars have been totally omitted. However No 15 still has its original windows and the terrace retains some, at least, of its former appeal.

PRINCE STREET – *east side*

Victoria Hall 1887

This has been an important building in the social life of the town for well over 100 years, providing a venue for lectures, dances and events such as "The Pleasantries and Working Exhibition of Local Industries" held here at Easter 1892. The upper facade of the Hall has some merit, particularly the large plaques (of cast iron?) which proclaim the name and date. That photo also demonstrates the softness of the local brick. Lower down it is all very cluttered. Perhaps visually the best part of the building is the back, where the curved brickwork rears up into a sail like gable, reminiscent of the Sydney Opera House!

79

Chapter 15 - NORTH STREET - west side

47 North Street (photo on p77)
This compact corner shop with cut away doorway is linked with the former steam mill in New Street. The hipped roof of the shop, facing New Street, seems to have undergone major surgery at some point. The rear part of the roof is peg tiled, not slated. This suggests that although mid Victorian in appearance there may be an 18thC core to this building. In 1871 the baker, John Wilson, was living above the shop with his wife, Eliza, and their unmarried daughter, Phoebe. ß

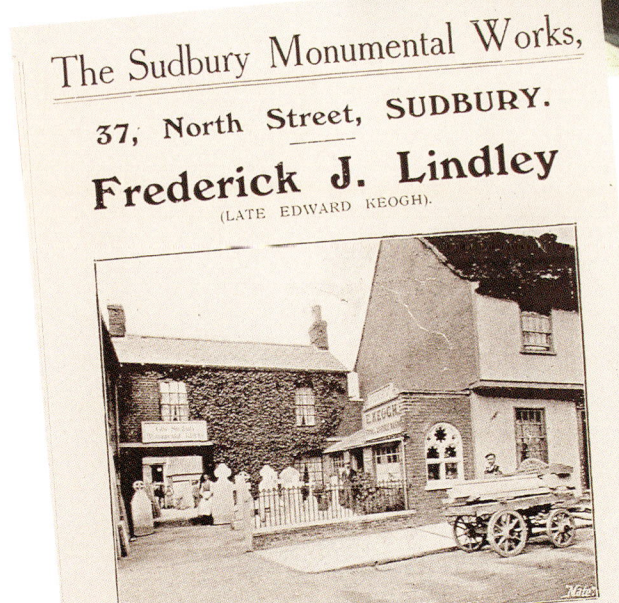

20-22 North Street
A well proportioned row of Victorian shops c1880. The detailing is restrained - just a line of moulded brick brackets supporting the eaves and a decorative string course with cable and nail head motifs copied from Norman architecture. A central passageway leads to the rear of the shops. The panelled pilasters give rhythm and unity to the three shopfronts, helping to counteract their contrasting paintwork.

37 North Street
This house, office and yard originally belonged to the stone mason, Edward Keogh; he was there in 1876 but had passed on by the date of the advertisement, 1906. The Gothic window to his office on the right was an appropriate way of demonstrating his stone carving skills. Many of the carved datestones we see on Victorian buildings around the town came from his workshop and of course his work can also be seen in the Cemetery. Today, it is highly appropriate that these premises are occupied by the local undertaker. A group of buildings which adds interest and variety to the townscape.

80

NORTH STREET - east side

North Street Tavern

There has been a public house here from at least 1844 when it was known as The Horn and Ambrose Sillitoe was the proprietor. However at the heart of the building is a much older timber framed core, perhaps 17thC, and a peg tiled cross wing also survives at the rear, (shown in the smaller photo). In the 19thC a second wing, of red brick and slate, was added at the rear, parallel to Suffolk Road, whilst the main building was raised to three storeys. The present two storey neo-Georgian facade dates from the 1960's.

64-65 North Street

This pair of properties was built in 1833 for Ambrose Prentice, Grocer and Tea Dealer. His initials are on the corner of No. 65 (on the right) and this may well have been his shop with his private house next door. The central blank window above the arched doorways would have been included to give regularity to the facade. The two modern shop fronts were inserted in the late 20thC. Whilst clearly a later addition, they harmonise well with the old building; it is very difficult to detect the joins between old and new bricks. However a clutter of modern signs and fire alarms has been added, disturbing the harmony of the facade.

81

NORTH STREET - *east side*

The Masonic Hall 1886

This hall and former hotel dominates the approach to Sudbury from the Melford Road. We are confident that it was built by Grimwood and Sons; the building bears many of the firm's stylistic trademarks, including a greenhouse on the roof! The building certainly makes a bold statement but the mix of different levels and styles combine somewhat uneasily. The same can be said of the doorways where stone, tile, brick and terracotta elements jostle together in the rich decoration. Modern replacement windows have been fitted but they replicate the glazing pattern of the former wooden windows.

Chapter 16 - GIRLING STREET to QUEENS ROAD

GIRLING STREET - east side

26 Girling Street

No 26 is a typical late Victorian terraced house. Of rather more interest is the two storey pantiled building at the rear, shown in the photo. This was one of a large number of local dairies existing in the 19th and early 20thC; indeed it was still common to see cattle being brought into the town for milking even after WW2. This particular dairy was owned in the early 20thC first by Albert Maylon and then by Thomas Hardacre. The milking parlour was on the left and the dairy itself on the right.

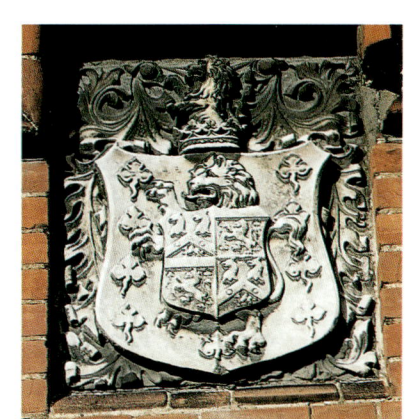

SUFFOLK ROAD - north side

15-17 Suffolk Road

This is a striking reinterpretation of medieval long wall jetty construction from the versatile local builder, Grimwood and Son. To fit two houses into this narrow site Grimwood built them back to back with the front doors in the side passageways. The upper floors are jettied to front and side, giving maximum space upstairs. The chimney is made into a feature, rising up through the tile-hung gable and decorated with a coat of arms, most probably fake. Not 1500 but around 1900 in date.

83

YORK ROAD – *south side*

St John's Methodist Church 1902

This is St John's Centenary year. The church was designed by Gunton, a partner in a London firm of architects specialising in civic and religious buildings. This might well be an Anglican church - a nave, transept, chancel and even an organ loft are included in the design. The split flints used for the walls contrast well with the red brick and Bath stone used for the dressings. The general style is Early English Gothic but the grand west window is a confident and harmonious mix of Decorated and Perpendicular. In passing note how difficult it is to get an uninterrupted view of this and indeed any building around this busy junction where five roads meet. We have counted 26 separate lamp posts, crossing beacons, signpost supports and other visual clutter.

Drain grating

This sits in the gutter outside the Church - the last drain before the junction with Melford Road. Some readers will doubtless find it strange that we include such a utilititarian object but it is a tangible link with the town's commercial past. Dupont and Orttewell Ltd. were recorded in Kelly's 1908 Directory as wholesale and retail ironmongers, bellhangers, acetylene & general gasfitters etc etc (the list is lengthy!). They were based at 55 Gainsborough Street, in Burkitt's Lane and in Bures and seem to have taken over the business of William Green. Clearly they were a fair sized firm yet this is the only identifiable example of their work that we have seen in the town.

YORK ROAD – south side

14 York Road, Craigmore

Coming from Melford Road No 14 acts as a visual full stop to the attractive row of semi detached villas Nos 2-12. Craigmore is no wider than its neighbours but has a long return frontage to Queens Road. Among many attractive original features are the rusticated stone segmental arch over the doorway and the front door itself with a floral pattern in the stained glass and an oriental feel to the wooden moulding below. It was built by Clement Dennington in about 1902 on land that had originally been acquired by the Fennell Brothers to build their silk mill but was surplus to their needs. The brothers made sure that there was a sale covenant preventing Dennington from building a silk mill of his own here. The Fennell mill was demolished in 1999.

QUEENS ROAD – west side

9-15 Queens Road

An innovative design from the Edwardian era in which the traditional pitched roof was replaced with a flat roof. This was cheaper to build and doubtless thought to be more in tune with the new century; however flat roofs never really caught on in this country, not least because of the problem of draining water off the roof. The rest of the design retains strong links with the 19thC in the handling of the bay windows and the use of local brick. The close up shows the attractive porch of No 13 which also retains its original front door. We believe that George Grimwood was the builder.

QUEENS ROAD – west side

97-99 Queens Road

Similar late 19th/early 20thC terraces exist in many roads to the north and east of the town centre. This pair have good proportions and retain their original wooden bays and sash windows - note the very small upper panes of stained glass. No 99 (on the right) still retains its original front door, again with small margin lights of stained glass. Such houses in near original condition are increasingly difficult to find in the town; we should celebrate those that remain.

WOODHALL ROAD - north side

The Steam Pump House 1872

This building was of key importance to the growth of the town in the late 19thC - it was essential to the expansion of housing up onto the eastern slopes of the Stour valley. The town's Waterworks was built here in 1872 at a cost of £8000. The 16 hp steam engine could pump up 16000 gallons of water an hour from the 300' deep underground borehole and along a pipe running beneath the footpath opposite to the covered reservoir at the top of York Road. From there gravity took the water down to supply the new housing development on the valley slopes below.

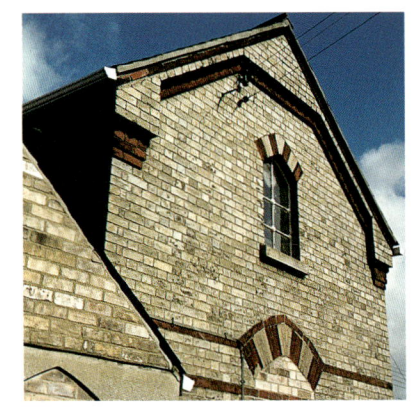

QUEENS ROAD – east side

The Mount, Queens Road

The house dates from the late 1870's. The porch and bays on the ground floor have a certain heavy grandeur but the house has been included not just for its looks but for its historical links with the large maltings which once lay just behind it. The house and maltings are first mentioned in an 1879 Directory which lists Alfred Spencer, Maltster. Spencer was followed by Frederick Goodall, Maltster and Merchant. The maltings has long gone, to be replaced by houses, but The Mount remains.

86

QUEENS ROAD – *east side*

HUMPHRY ROAD – *east side*

Edward VIII Pillar box (no.1088)
This pillar box outside 10/12 Humphry Road is said to be one of only six in the country and bears a crown that was never actually placed upon Edward's head. The box has recently been refurbished after many years of neglect which followed the closure of the shop and post office behind.

112 Queens Road, Woodburn
John Deeks of Sible Hedingham, Gentleman, had this house built in 1890. It has a great deal of visual interest - note the large two storey bay on the north side beneath a highly decorated gable, which creates the illusion that this was the real front of the house. The windows also repay attention - note the original sashes with floral keystones above and the very unusual moulded brick sills. The terracotta ridge tiles add a nice finishing touch.

87

Chapter 17 - MELFORD ROAD - west side

The west side of Melford Road, backing onto North Meadow, was developed in the late 1850's/early 1860's. The properties are mainly terraced, initially set back from the road with front gardens and then, beyond the Bay Horse PH, directly fronting onto the pavement. In Victorian times this was a semi autonomous, mainly working class, community with three public houses, two dairies and a range of shops supplying basic needs; many of the houses were also places of work. This was referred to locally as the "sixpenny side" of the road as opposed to the "shilling side" - the long row of middle class villas opposite.

1-7 Melford Road, (Louth Villas)

This group of four substantial, well proportioned villas was constructed by the builder, FW Jennings, in the early 1880's on a field formerly known as Round Croft. Jennings' initials are on the plaque. These are large family homes built for people of some means. It is interesting that the terrace was only integrated into the numbering system of Melford Road in the 1960's; perhaps indicative that the residents did not see themselves as part of the "sixpenny" terraces on that side of Melford Road! Although No 3 has some replacement windows the terrace retains many original features; note the wooden porches with trellis work decoration and the conservatory at the side of No1 - shown in the detail on the right. Additional visual interest is provided by the decoration on the carved stone lintels and the dogtooth and cable moulding on the continuous string course.

9-15 Melford Road

These two adjacent pairs of villas were built about 1860 by Grimwoods, most probably for rent rather than sale. The general view above shows Alpha Villas (Nos 9-11) which have their original slate roof and front doors. In the 1861 Census Charles Keogh, the stone mason, lived at No 9 and William Bentley, the Baptist minister, at No 11. A wine cellarman and a retired woollen draper lived in the other pair. The decoration on the ground floor catches the eye; cement has been moulded to form the brackets supporting both the window architraves and the very striking arches around each pair of front doors. The doorway of Alpha Villas features a central lionhead motif; whilst the detail photo shows the foliate mask motif shared by Nos 13-15.

MELFORD ROAD – *west side*

17-27 Melford Road, Victoria Terrace 1858

A very early development by George Grimwood and clearly moving further down the social scale from the properties we have seen so far. Among the artisans resident there in 1861 there were a tinman, carpenter, tailor and butcher. Sadly only No 23 (illustrated) retains its original sashes and some of the other houses have very inappropriate replacement windows. However the attractive paired doorways, each with a blank window above, and the general good proportions justify the inclusion of the whole terrace for group value. The bricks have acquired an interesting patina over the past 150 years; cleaning or painting the brickwork of one house would destroy the unity of the whole terrace.

41 Melford Road

These two buildings are closely associated with the local silk industry. The house at right angles to the road frontage was the foreman or manager's house. In 1861 Benjamin Brown, silk umbrella foreman, lived here with his wife Elizabeth, a silk winder, and his two young boys, Josiah and William. Down the side, what appears to be a garage is actually part of the two storey silk factory which survived more or less intact until the 1970's. The house and factory were built by Kipling, Pain and Co. which, like most of the local silk firms, originated in the Spitalfields area of London. In the early 20thC the factory was occupied by a firm of corset and staymakers and then a local cabinet makers.

89

MELFORD ROAD – west side

67 Melford Road

This is the first of the weavers' cottages which extend from here northward along the road. In 1861 James Wheeler, dealer in stock, lived here and again in 1871, when he was described as a toll collector. By 1881 it had become a butcher's shop presided over by his son(?) Edward Wheeler. His shopfront is a rare survival. Meat could be hung on the iron rail and the overhanging canopy gave some protection from the elements although none from flies and the dust thrown up by passing traffic! Note the large sash window which could be raised to reveal the display counter behind.

75-79 Melford Road

Another good group of late Victorian shop frontages inserted into three former weavers' cottages. No 77 (the right hand of the blue painted properties) was linked for many years as one shop with No 79 (yellow paint, Sasha). They share one continuous frontage with identical carving on the brackets at each end. Initially they were separately occupied by weavers but by 1891 the two houses had been combined to become the premises of Edward Wheeler, furniture dealer. He was another member of the Wheeler dynasty which once owned most of the properties in this part of the road. By 1908 A.J.Beer, a decorator, had his premises here and his faded sign can still just be made out on the brickwork. The history of No 75 (left hand, blue painted) still needs unravelling; it has an elegant shop frontage, clearly designed to complement those to the right.

90

MELFORD ROAD – west side

81 Melford Road

By 1881 these two former silk weavers' cottages had been converted into a grocer's shop run by James Wheeler; by 1912 it was also the local sub post office. Doubtless there has been some restoration to the shopfront over the years but the wooden architrave with supporting brackets at each end looks original and the general proportions are excellent. One late Victorian sash survives on the first floor but there are now none of the small paned windows characteristic of mid Victorian weavers' cottages.

83 Melford Road

This two storey house is contemporary with the weavers cottages on either side. In 1861 a dye works foreman lived here but by 1871 Alfred Murton, miller and baker, was in residence. The property remained a bakery for many years; Caleb Pegrum was the baker here in 1922. Clearly the present shop front contains two modern doors on the left but the overall framework and the stained glass shop door could well date back to the late 19thC. We welcome the hand painted sign on the brickwork, reviving an old practice.

91 Melford Road

No 91 is the right hand of a pair of weavers' cottages. On the top floor is a rare local example of a "Yorkshire" sash window (sliding horizontally, not vertically) which must date from the time in 1861 when William Edey worked at his loom on the first floor below. However the conventional sash window on that floor and the large ground floor sash window beneath its heavy stone lintel are both late Victorian insertions, probably dating from when it became a grocer's shop in the 1890's. By 1912 No 91 had become the premises of George Beevis, pork butcher. A building of considerable visual interest.

MELFORD ROAD – west side

131 Melford Road

No 131 forms part of St Gregory's Terrace, a group of four weavers' cottages "erected and built by one Azariah Clubb" in 1860 on part of Long Croft "situate to the west side of the turnpike road from Sudbury to Melford". Clubb was himself a weaver but also a parish clerk and clearly a man of some enterprise. No 131 is important today because it is the only such cottage in the whole road which retains its original windows. On the top floor is a casement window. Below, the first floor loom shop stretched right through the the property so that large windows at each end could shed maximum light on the loom; note the small four pane opening casement set within the larger window. William Davis senior was the first weaver to ply his trade here, collecting his warp beam and bobbins of silk from his master's manufactory and, after many arduous hours of labour, returning the woven roll of silk to be weighed and inspected for quality. Only then was he paid and given fresh supplies.

Sudbury Hall, Melford Road

This imposing, mid 19thC mansion was formerly known as Holgate House and then Arthur Hall. In 1864 Walter Poley Esq. lived here, a JP and a man of substance! Both the entrance porch, supported by pilasters and columns, and the turret above add visual interest to a rather severe looking building. The house has been re-windowed and it is difficult to know how far these modern windows replicate the original glazing pattern. Despite this the house and out buildings form an attractive grouping on the northern approach to the town, complemented by the long, white brick panelled boundary wall fronting onto Melford Road and Brundon Lane.

MELFORD ROAD – west side

Chapter 18 - MELFORD ROAD - east side

The high ground to the east of Melford Road became available for housing rather later than on the west side; indeed houses might never have been built at all if the original plan to construct the railway along this route had been carried out.

Between York Road and Woodhall Road the steep slope above the road is dominated by an imposing row of late Victorian and Edwardian villas - the family homes of a comfortably off middle class. A significant number of these properties were occupied by successful local shopkeepers, no longer living over the family shop.

The early photo c1906 shows these houses sitting comfortably behind their garden walls and wrought iron gates with not a lampost or overhead wire in sight. Much of this vista remains and we list the whole row because it is still an important element in the Sudbury townscape. However what a difference it would make if the forest of overhead wires could be buried underground. Six properties have been chosen as a reasonably representative sample to illustrate the whole vista between York Road and the pair of villas flanking the entrance to Woodhall Road.

The Holgate, Melford Road

The house stands on a steep slope looking across the fields to Bulmer and some 200 metres from the roundabout which marks the end of Melford Road. The high and rather narrow, small paned sash windows suggest a date around 1840-50 and census records indeed show that by 1851 the house was occupied by the family of Jonathan Grubb, bank agent. However in places foundations of flint and red brick are visible beneath the present white brick walls. These could well belong to a former building on the site, possibly The Sudbury Arms, an inn which stood hereabouts in the 18thC next to a tollgate. The large expanse of white brickwork on the Holgate is offset by the deep eaves and by the way in which each pair of windows is set inside a recessed panel in the brickwork. The dignified porch supported by Roman Doric columns is a modern addition but it is in keeping with the house.

MELFORD ROAD – *east side*
Nos 4-74 Melford Road - Listed for group value

10-12 Melford Road

These grand detached villas have been well maintained in their original condition over the past 100 years. They share a certain superficial similarity, particularly at eaves and roof level, but note the very different designs of the bay windows. It is unclear who built them because builder's names are only mentioned in title deeds if they actually owned the plot but Clement Dennington is the likely builder. Dennington built many other houses in the road including his own house, No 22, Orford House, which he named after his birthplace. No 10 (on the right) was built c1896 for Henry Smith, bootmaker, with the assistance of a mortgage loan from his son, the watchmaker and jeweller, Angelo Smith. In 1901 it was "to let" but next door No 12 was occupied by the baker, Frederick Ulmer, and his family. During the Zeppelin raids of 1916 rumours began to circulate that he was a German spy and he moved to London, leaving his English wife to manage their bakery in Old Bakery Mews, King Street.

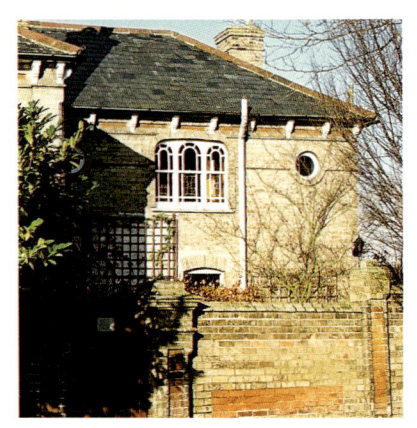

4 Melford Road, Northfield House

No 4 was built at the same time as Nos 6 and 8 with which it shares a common wall and many stylistic features - the inset red brick panels in the wall are repeated elsewhere on the facades and chimneys of all three houses. The moulded brick detailing around the door arch and the window jambs of No 4 is a subtle and expensive feature and its rear wing has an attractive stained glass, triple arched sash window. All three houses were erected by the builder, Edward Salter of Chilton, c1870, on land originally part of the Woodhall Farm Estate. In 1901 two spinster sisters, Phoebe and Mary Wright, lived at No 4, with Joseph Hills, a retired postmaster at No 6 and John Burlingham, a retired farmer, at No 8.

MELFORD ROAD – *east side*

44-46 Melford Road

Another fine pair of villas but this time semi detached. In 1889 William Smith, gentleman, acquired this plot for £77 10/-. Subsequently he had No 44 Prior Villa (right) and No 46 Stour Villa (left) built on the land and he then rented out the properties. In 1901 Thomas Haywood, the Borough Engineer Surveyor, was living at Prior Villa and Harriet Wheeler, widow, lived on her own means at Stour Villa. These villas have strong stylistic links with No 10 Melford Road and were almost certainly built by Dennington. The pair work well together, serenely dominating the road below, but pity the poor postman!

50 Melford Road, The Laurels

This house is on the extreme left in the early photo taken in 1906 (see p93) and is still a commanding presence in the road, occupying a particularly wide plot. However this enabled the construction, a few years back, of a driveway which led to the removal of part of the original front wall on the right hand side. The elaborate cast iron gate survives together with the walls and pillars flanking the ascent up to the front door, clearly intended to impress. The different treatment of the two bays is noteworthy, the wider one gabled, the other hipped. The detail photo shows how each double sash window is divided by a delicate stone column - a delightful and expensive decorative feature. Likely to be another Dennington house.

MELFORD ROAD – east side

66 Melford Road
This is one of a small group of red brick Edwardian villas which serve as a attractive counterpoint to the dominant Suffolk white brick in the road. Superficially all four seem similar but there are subtle differences in the arches above doors and windows. All were erected by Clement Dennington, c1906. The intricate floral detailing of the stonework around the door and window arches is very well preserved, suggesting that this is real stone rather than cheaper moulded cement. The wooden bay window on the ground floor is a characteristic Edwardian feature, easily assembled from mass produced parts supplied by builders' merchants.

72 Melford Road, The Limes
This is another Dennington house, part of a larger land holding which first came on the market in 1867 and subsequently passed through the hands of various gentleman investors before Dennington bought the plot for £232 10/- in 1906. He sold the completed house in 1907 to John Cuckmore of Hartest, grocer, for £515. There were major changes at the design stage; the house we see bears no relation to the plans lodged with the Borough Council but, thankfully, what we see is a far more interesting building. The intricate pattern of the glazing bars in the upper part of each window has an almost Moorish look, whilst the moulded bricks forming the lintels seem inspired by Norman beakhead decoration. At the eaves a row of carved modillions supports the overhang of a very extensive slate roof.

MELFORD ROAD – east side

Beyond Woodhall Road there are a number of inter-war houses and bungalows. We then come to this group of large detached houses, enjoying uninterrupted views across North Meadow.

102 Melford Road, Prospect House

This substantial house must have stood in isolation for many years before the adjacent plots were developed. The front is rendered but underneath it is probably white brick; red brick is used at the sides and rear. The small paned sashes and dignified good looks suggest a mid 19thC date, although the gabled oriel window may well be a later Edwardian addition. The flanking Chile pines are very characteristic of large Victorian gardens, bringing in an exotic touch. Dr John Holden, the Borough Medical Officer, lived here in 1879 and a Mr Michael George in 1896. By 1901 his widow(?), Amelia George, seems to have been living in this large house on her own with just one servant, a 16 year old housemaid, Emily Claydon.

104 Melford Road, Inward House

Built in 1890 by Grimwood and Sons and designed by their architect and eventual head of the firm, Arthur Grimwood (1851-1918). Arthur was a qualified architect who had trained both in London and on the Continent. His own highly distinctive and unique style can be seen to advantage here. Note the projecting twin gables carried on brackets, each gable containing the house name or date picked out in plaster. On the first floor the balustrade is a prominent feature, linking the two bays and serving to shelter the entrance porch below. There is also an attractive semi circular stained glass panel above the outer door.

MELFORD ROAD – east side

110 Melford Road, Coombe Vale

This substantial double bayed house dates from 1908 and it is interesting to compare it with No 104, built 18 years earlier. There is a strong family resemblance in the design of the two houses but here red pantiles are used, perhaps working less well with the white brick, the gables are smaller and the roof is less steeply pitched. The house featured in a contemporary advertisement for Grimwood's "Priory Estate" and the facade has changed very little since then: although the dormer window looks to be a later insertion, it is in fact an original feature.

112 Melford Road, Abbey House

This is yet another Grimwood house of 1911, which Arthur Grimwood built for his manager, James McQuae, and his wife Nancy. They lived there for some seven years before moving to 1 Church Walk to take over the business on Arthur's death. The house has many interesting and striking features, in particular the central projecting wing with a massive bressumer beam on heavy brackets supporting the oriel window above. Also note how arched braces have been inserted to support the cut away right hand corner of the house - another highly individual touch. All this appears to be functional timberwork, not the more usual mock Tudor "applique"!

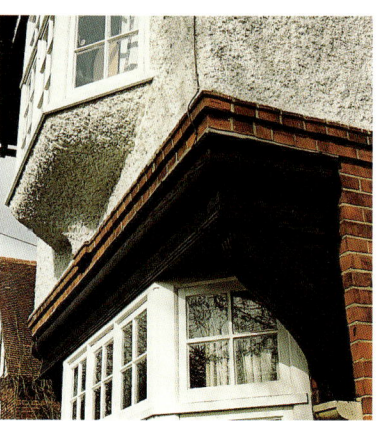

MELFORD ROAD – east side

118 & 120 Melford Road

Stour View (right) and Abbots Ford (left) are the newly built houses featured in this Grimwood advertisement of 1906. The identities of the two gentlemen in boaters is unknown; perhaps one of them is Arthur Grimwood or possibly the first occupier of Stour View, Lt. Col. David Semple MD RAMC. With the roof gardens and basements these are actually five storey properties. They have changed very little since they were built on "the finest site in England" and the view from the roof gardens remains truly spectacular. However one change is obvious, the removal of the entrance arch, although the two-tone pillars with supporting stone scrolls remain. (Incidentally similar pillars can be seen flanking the Acton Square entrance to the Grimwood-owned Waggon and Horses PH.) All Grimwood houses have individuality; the greenhouses on the roof of this particular pair make them unique!

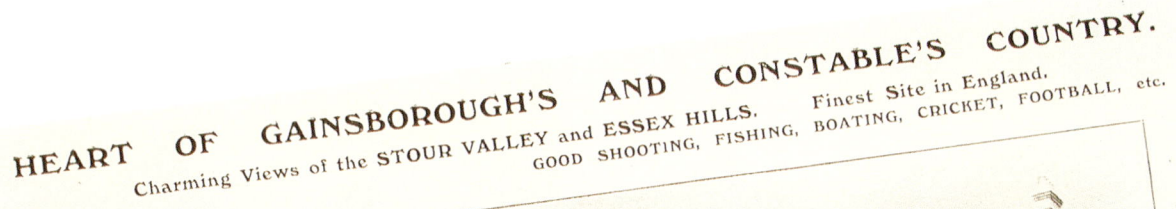

HEART OF GAINSBOROUGH'S AND CONSTABLE'S COUNTRY.

Charming Views of the STOUR VALLEY and ESSEX HILLS. Finest Site in England.

GOOD SHOOTING, FISHING, BOATING, CRICKET, FOOTBALL, etc.

The **PRIORY ESTATE**, Near SUDBURY, SUFFOLK.

Semi-detached **BIJOUX VILLAS**

Artistically finished inside and out, containing 5 Bedrooms, Bathroom (with hot and cold water), Drawing Room, Dining Room, Kitchen, Scullery, and every convenience. Roof Gardens. Freedom from Motor Dust.

TO BE SOLD OR LET. Rent very moderate. Sites also for Sale.

Rates Very Low. No Borough Charges. Parish of St. Bartholomew, the smallest in England.

GEO. GRIMWOOD & SONS, Builders, SUDBURY.

MELFORD ROAD – east side

132-134 Melford Road

This pair of back to back cottages is replicated by Nos 128-130 (on the other side of the entrance to Colneys Close). They stand on the site of the Hospital of St Leonard, founded in the reign of Edward II by John Colney as a leper hospital. He suffered from the terrible affliction himself and retired there to become its first governor. By the 19thC it was proving difficult to find residents, even by widening the definition to include serious skin complaints, and in 1858 the Hospital buildings and land passed into the hands of the Municipal Charity Trustees. The old hospital was pulled down and they then erected "two detached double tenements near the site of the old buildings at a cost of £376". The exact building date is uncertain but about 1865 and the rents went to the support of the new St Leonard's Cottage Hospital. Each pair of simple cottages was built back to back although each individual plot had a large garden. Inevitably these four cottages became known as "Leprosy Cottages": indeed they are named as such in the 1901 Census when they were rented out to various labouring men - farm labourers and mat makers. The cottages are quite attractive in themselves but also form an interesting link with the town's distant past.

Chapter 19 - PRIORY ROAD – north side

7-13 Priory Road, St Olaves 1908

The style of this short terrace is less ornate and baroque than the villas that Grimwoods built on the Melford Road. The advertisement refers to them as "ENGLISH HOMES OLD YET NEW" and they clearly draw on the English vernacular tradition with their tile hung gables and jettied cross wings. Hot and cold running water was part of the "new" appeal of these properties. No 9 has suffered some alterations to its first floor window and gable but overall the terrace still looks much as it did back in 1908 when the photographer stood in the meadow opposite.

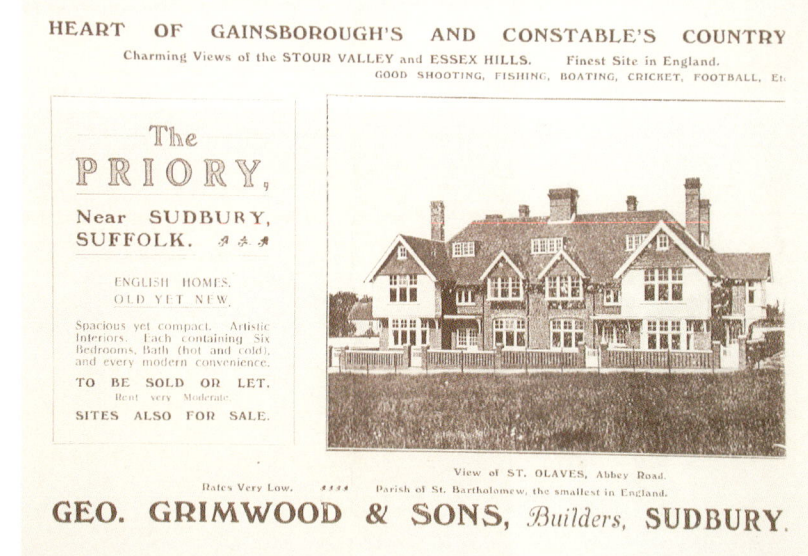

PRIORY ROAD – north side

15-17 Priory Road, Greyfriars 1907

This pair is in great contrast to the flanking Grimwood properties, further evidence, if it is still needed, of the firm's versatility. The flat roofed design was highly innovative and had many advantages, particularly the saving on expensive roof trusses and slates or tiles. However in the long run it never really caught on in domestic architecture, perhaps a combination of water penetration problems and English conservatism. The absence of a conventional roof is actually not all that noticeable here with various devices used, such as the two bands of red brick and the deep overhang of the eaves, to create the illusion of a roof.

19 Priory Road

Yet another Grimwood house c1908. The story is that Arthur Grimwood went on holiday to Switzerland and came back inspired to build a Swiss chalet in Priory Road. In fact there are many influences at work in this building including the classical - note the two attractive arched windows with stained glass margin lights. However, there is a Swiss influence at work in the alignment of the axis of the roof at 90 degrees to the road, the deep overhang of the eaves and the first floor balcony and window shutters. Arthur Grimwood may have picked up the idea for the chimney stacks disguised as turrets in Italy; they certainly add the finishing touch to a highly individual and visually enjoyable building.

101

SUDBURY

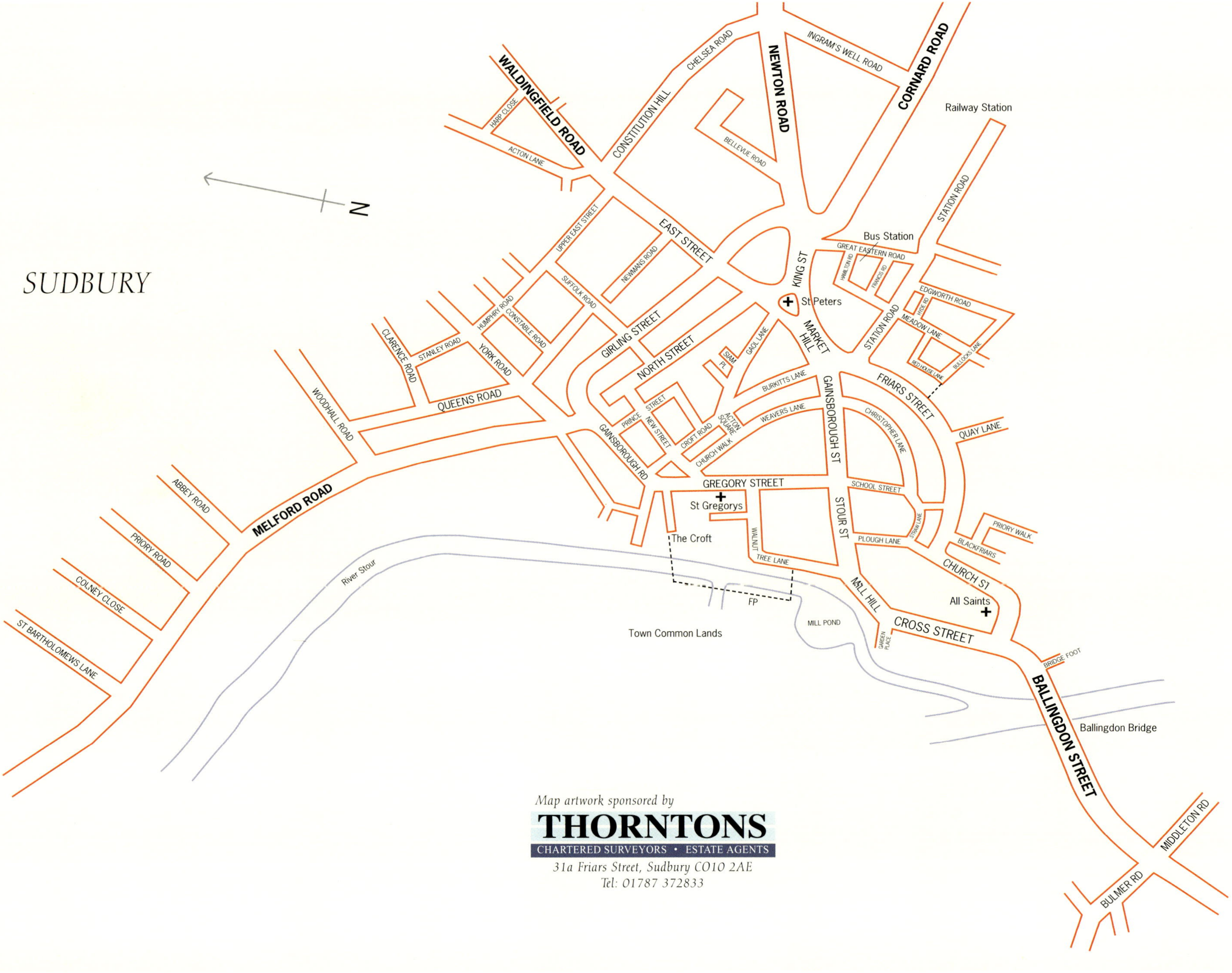

Map artwork sponsored by

THORNTONS
CHARTERED SURVEYORS • ESTATE AGENTS
31a Friars Street, Sudbury CO10 2AE
Tel: 01787 372833

INDEX OF PROPERTIES

	pages		pages
ACTON SQUARE 3-6;8-10;11 (Dental Emporium)	72-73	CROSS STREET – E side: 5-9;30-31;32; Bull Inn (return frontage);36;37;38 – W side: 61;82-83; summerhouses to Nos79&85;Spread Eagle PH;102	9-14
BALLINGDON ST – SE side: Horse Trough (by railway bridge);21-22;24(Forge House); 47-48(Talas House.);51-53 – NW side: Red Onion;67;68-70; Refuse/Sewage Works	5-8	EAST STREET – N side: White Horse stables; 2(Queensbury);7-8;12-14;20; 29; Horse & Groom PH;Eastgate House. – S side: 48-51;88-89(Diapers)	51-54
BANK BUILDINGS 2-8	37		
BELLEVUE ROAD 13(Homeland)	48	EDGWORTH ROAD 1-2(Stour Valley Villas); 3 (Primrose Cottage)	42
BRIDGE FOOT 5	12		
BRUNDON LANE Stone Cottage (adjacent to Brundon Hall)	4	FRIARS STREET – SE side:1-3;19(Bentley House); 47;Cricket ground railings;63 – NW side: 8(Banyan);8C;10-12(Kestrel); 22(Moore Green);Vict PO box(adj.58B);70	26-30
BULMER ROAD 7(End Cottage);10;14	2-3		
BURKITTS LANE Black Boy PH stables; 9-12;21-22	70-71	GAINSBOROUGH ROAD 8-10	78
CHURCH STREET – SE side: 8-11;32-33 – NW side: 37-42(All Saints Terrace);44;46; Baptist Church;49-50;54	17-20	GAINSBOROUGH ST – N side: Drill Hall;48 (Norway Hse);49;50-52 – S side: 2-4;9;milestone(adj.16); 20(Bradbury Courtyard)	61-63
CHURCH WALK Waggon& Horses PH; Wall of 1890;1;2-4;6	68-69	GAOL LANE – W side: 21;21a(warehouses); 23(Toymaster);25-39;47-49;Wall to Siam Gdns	59-60
CORNARD ROAD – W side: 1-6;22-24; Stephen Walters mill – E side: 55;57	46-48	GARDEN PLACE 8	8
THE CROFT 1-5;28 & North House; mosaic wall (Croft Cottage); drain grating (adj.the Convent)	65-67	GIRLING STREET 26(former dairy at rear)	83
		GT EASTERN ROAD Nettas Drycleaners;weighbridge	46
CROFT ROAD 1-4(Gardenside)	74	GREGORY STREET Pentecostal Church;Gregory Mills	63

103

	pages
HUMPHRY ROAD *Ed.VIII PO box(adj.10)*	87
MARKET HILL *45(HSBC);* *water fountain/trough(by church)*	58
MEADOW LANE *1;2(Meadow Lodge)* *Former Gasworks offices at W end*	34-35
MELFORD ROAD – W side: *1-7(Louth Villas);9-15;17-27* *(Victoria Terrace);41;67;75-79;81;83;91;131;* *Sudbury Hall;The Holgate* – E side: *(4-74 listed for grp. val.)4;10-12;* *44-46;50(Laurels);66;72;102* *(Prospect House);104(Inward House);* *110(Coombe Vale);112(Abbey House);* *118-120;132-134*	88-93 93-100
MIDDLETON ROAD *11-41*	2
MILL HILL *27(Hill House)*	14
NEWMANS ROAD *18-20;28-34*	57
NEW STREET – S side: *1-6;Chapel;* *7(Rare Books);10-11;15-18;* – N side: *21-23;26-28;New Hall;* *Mill(pt.of 47Nth.St.)*	74-78
NEWTON ROAD – N side: *7(Chelsea Lodge);* *Cemetery gates, wall & chapels* – S side: *Belle Vue;Oakdene & Ventnor*	49-50
NORTH STREET – W side:*20-22;* *37(Brown Fenn);47* – E side: *Masonic Hall;64-65;North St Tavern*	80-82

	pages
OLD MARKET PLACE *10(Edin.Wool Shop)*	58
PLOUGH LANE – E side: *(1-7 grp.val.) 7* – W side: *(21-36 grp.val.);21;22-24*	20-22
PRINCE STREET *11-18(Girton Terrace);* *Victoria Hall*	78-79
PRIORY ROAD *7-13;15-17;19*	100-101
PRIORY WALK *The Old Priory;* *factory on E side*	31
QUAY LANE *1;4;Pavilion;Boathouse*	32-33
QUEENS ROAD – E side: *The Mount;112* – W side: *9-15;97-99*	85-87
RED HOUSE LANE *The Cottage(adj.Red House)*	4
SCHOOL STREET *1;14-24;36*	25
SIAM PLACE *3*	60
STATION ROAD – E side *Warehouses to rear 38 Market Hill;* *Kingdom Hall;Oak Lodge;10-11;14-15;* *Easterns PH* – W side: *36-38(Railway Bell/Bruntons);* *39-40;drain grating (adj.43);* *50;51;52);53;54-55(old FP offices);57-9*	36-45
STOUR STREET *Kentish Lodge*	16
STRAW LANE *Ivy Lodge;Coach House;2-5;* *Trap House;8-11*	22-24

	pages
SUFFOLK ROAD *15-17*	83
VALLEY WALK/BRUNDON LANE *Railway bridge*	4
WALDINGFIELD ROAD *1-3;19;35-37;39;43;57*	55-57
WALNUTTREE LANE *Riverside Cottage;* *39(Granary);Walnuttree Hospital*	15-16
WEAVERS LANE *Iron gate adj. Print Workshop*	70
WOODHALL ROAD *Former Waterworks pump house*	82
YORK ROAD *St Johns Methodist Church;* *adj. drain grating;14*	84-85